50 Japanese Premium Dish Recipes for Home

By: Kelly Johnson

Table of Contents

- Sushi (Various Types)
- Sashimi Platter
- Tempura
- Sukiyaki
- Shabu-Shabu
- Chirashi Sushi
- Tonkatsu
- Okonomiyaki
- Yakitori
- Miso Soup with Clams
- Udon Noodles with Tempura
- Teriyaki Chicken
- Grilled Mackerel with Miso
- Kaiseki Ryori (Traditional Multi-course Meal)
- Oden (Japanese Hot Pot)
- Yakiniku (Japanese BBQ)
- Chawanmushi (Steamed Egg Custard)
- Takoyaki (Octopus Balls)
- Gyoza (Japanese Dumplings)
- Unagi Don (Grilled Eel Rice Bowl)
- Katsudon (Pork Cutlet Rice Bowl)
- Ramen (Various Types)
- Oyakodon (Chicken and Egg Rice Bowl)
- Nikujaga (Meat and Potato Stew)
- Hiyashi Chuka (Cold Ramen Salad)
- Ankimo (Monkfish Liver)
- Agedashi Tofu (Deep Fried Tofu)
- Matsutake Gohan (Matsutake Rice)
- Chashu (Roasted Pork)
- Natto (Fermented Soybeans)
- Fugu (Blowfish)
- Kakiage (Mixed Vegetable Tempura)
- Hiroshima Okonomiyaki
- Tai Sashimi (Sea Bream Sashimi)
- Kani Miso (Crab Miso Soup)

- Ika Geso Karaage (Deep Fried Squid Tentacles)
- Zaru Soba (Cold Buckwheat Noodles)
- Yudofu (Tofu Hot Pot)
- Shojin Ryori (Buddhist Vegetarian Cuisine)
- Dashi (Japanese Soup Stock)
- Mitarashi Dango (Sweet Rice Dumplings)
- Hambagu (Japanese Hamburger Steak)
- Kaiseki Ryori (Traditional Multi-course Meal)
- Hamachi Kama (Yellowtail Collar)
- Chirashizushi (Scattered Sushi)
- Yakisoba (Stir-Fried Noodles)
- Matcha (Green Tea) Desserts
- Wagashi (Traditional Japanese Sweets)
- Sunomono (Cucumber Salad)
- Dorayaki (Red Bean Pancakes)

Sushi (Various Types)

Ingredients:

For Sushi Rice:

- 2 cups sushi rice
- 2 cups water
- 1/4 cup rice vinegar
- 2 tablespoons sugar
- 1 teaspoon salt

For Nigiri Sushi:

- Sushi rice (prepared as per instructions)
- Sashimi-grade fish (e.g., tuna, salmon, yellowtail)
- Wasabi paste
- Soy sauce

For Tekka Maki (Tuna Roll):

- Sushi rice (prepared as per instructions)
- 2-3 sheets nori (seaweed)
- 1/2 lb sushi-grade tuna, sliced into strips
- 1 avocado, thinly sliced
- 1/2 cucumber, julienned
- Soy sauce, pickled ginger, and wasabi for serving

For California Rolls:

- Sushi rice (prepared as per instructions)
- 2-3 sheets nori (seaweed)
- 1/2 lb imitation crab meat, shredded
- 1 avocado, thinly sliced
- 1/2 cucumber, julienned
- Sesame seeds (optional)
- Soy sauce, pickled ginger, and wasabi for serving

Instructions:

1. Prepare Sushi Rice:

- Rinse the sushi rice in cold water until the water runs clear.
- Combine the rice and water in a rice cooker or pot. Cook according to the rice cooker's instructions or bring to a boil, then cover and simmer for 15-20 minutes until the water is absorbed.

- In a small saucepan, heat the rice vinegar, sugar, and salt over low heat until dissolved. Remove from heat.
- Transfer the cooked rice to a large bowl and gently fold in the vinegar mixture using a wooden spoon or rice paddle. Allow the rice to cool to room temperature.

2. Make Nigiri Sushi:

- Wet your hands with water and lightly shake off excess. Take a small amount of sushi rice and gently press it into an oval shape with your fingers.
- Place a small dab of wasabi on top of the rice.
- Top with a slice of fish, pressing it gently onto the rice.
- Serve nigiri sushi with soy sauce and pickled ginger.

3. Make Tekka Maki (Tuna Roll):

- Place a bamboo sushi mat on a flat surface and cover it with plastic wrap.
- Lay a sheet of nori on the mat. Wet your hands and spread a thin layer of sushi rice evenly over the nori, leaving a 1-inch border at the top.
- Arrange strips of tuna, avocado slices, and cucumber along the bottom edge of the nori.
- Using the bamboo mat, roll the sushi tightly away from you, pressing gently to seal. Wet the top border of the nori to seal the roll.
- Slice the roll into 6-8 pieces using a sharp knife dipped in water. Repeat with remaining nori and filling ingredients.

4. Make California Rolls:

- Follow the same steps as Tekka Maki, but substitute the tuna with shredded imitation crab meat.
- Add avocado slices and cucumber strips along with the crab meat before rolling.
- Optionally, sprinkle sesame seeds on the rice before rolling for added texture and flavor.

5. Serve:

- Arrange the sushi rolls and nigiri on a plate.
- Serve with soy sauce, pickled ginger, and wasabi on the side.
- Enjoy your homemade sushi!

Tips:

- **Quality Ingredients:** Use fresh, high-quality fish and vegetables for best results.
- **Preparation:** Keep hands and utensils moistened when handling sushi rice to prevent sticking.
- **Technique:** Practice rolling sushi tightly and evenly to create neat rolls.
- **Variations:** Feel free to experiment with different fillings and toppings to create your favorite sushi combinations.

Enjoy making and eating your homemade sushi!

Sashimi Platter

Ingredients:

- **Assorted Sashimi Fish:** Choose a variety of sashimi-grade fish such as tuna (maguro), salmon (sake), yellowtail (hamachi), seabream (tai), and any other favorites.
- **Garnishes:** Optional garnishes can include daikon radish sprouts (kaiware), shiso leaves, cucumber slices, lemon wedges, and edible flowers for decoration.
- **Condiments:** Soy sauce (shoyu), wasabi paste, and pickled ginger (gari).

Instructions:

1. Prepare the Fish:

- Purchase sashimi-grade fish from a reputable fishmonger or Japanese market. It's essential that the fish is fresh and safe for raw consumption.
- Rinse the fish under cold water and pat dry with paper towels. Use a sharp knife to slice the fish thinly and evenly. Slice against the grain to ensure a smooth texture.
- Arrange the sliced fish on a plate or a wooden platter, keeping each type of fish separate to preserve its individual flavor.

2. Arrange the Platter:

- Start with larger pieces of sashimi in the center of the platter and arrange smaller pieces around them.
- Add garnishes such as daikon radish sprouts, shiso leaves, cucumber slices, and lemon wedges around the sashimi for color and freshness.
- Optionally, decorate with edible flowers or small pieces of nori (seaweed) for an elegant presentation.

3. Serve with Condiments:

- Place small dishes of soy sauce, wasabi paste, and pickled ginger on the platter or alongside it for guests to add according to their preference.
- Ensure there are small, individual serving plates and chopsticks for each guest.

4. Presentation Tips:

- Arrange the sashimi slices neatly and symmetrically for an aesthetically pleasing presentation.
- Use a wooden or ceramic platter for an authentic touch, as these materials complement the delicate flavors of the sashimi.

5. Enjoy:

- Sashimi is typically enjoyed as an appetizer or part of a larger Japanese meal. Encourage guests to savor each type of fish with different condiments to experience varying flavors and textures.

Notes:

- **Safety:** Ensure that all utensils and surfaces are clean when handling raw fish. Refrigerate sashimi-grade fish until ready to serve.
- **Variations:** Experiment with different types of fish and garnishes to create unique sashimi platters tailored to your preferences and seasonal availability.

Creating a sashimi platter at home allows you to enjoy the freshness and delicate flavors of high-quality fish in a traditional Japanese style.

Tempura

Ingredients:

- **For Tempura Batter:**
    - 1 cup all-purpose flour
    - 1/2 cup cornstarch
    - 1 teaspoon baking powder
    - 1 cup ice-cold water
    - Ice cubes
- **For Tempura Ingredients:**
    - Assorted seafood (shrimp, squid, fish fillets) and vegetables (zucchini, sweet potato, bell pepper, broccoli florets, mushrooms)
    - Oil for deep frying (vegetable oil or canola oil)
- **For Serving:**
    - Tempura dipping sauce (Tentsuyu):
        - 1/2 cup dashi (Japanese fish stock) or water
        - 1/4 cup soy sauce
        - 2 tablespoons mirin (sweet rice wine)
        - 1 tablespoon sugar
        - Optional garnish: grated daikon radish, grated ginger

Instructions:

1. Prepare the Tempura Batter:

- In a large bowl, sift together the all-purpose flour, cornstarch, and baking powder.
- Gradually add ice-cold water to the flour mixture, whisking gently until just combined. The batter should be slightly lumpy and thinner than pancake batter.
- Place a few ice cubes in the batter to keep it cold, which helps create a crispy texture.

2. Prepare the Tempura Ingredients:

- Prepare the seafood and vegetables by cutting them into bite-sized pieces. Ensure seafood is cleaned and patted dry with paper towels.
- Heat oil in a deep fryer or large pot to 340-350°F (170-180°C). Use enough oil to submerge the ingredients completely.

3. Coat and Fry the Tempura:

- Dip each piece of seafood or vegetable into the tempura batter, allowing excess batter to drip off.
- Carefully place the battered pieces into the hot oil, frying a few pieces at a time to maintain the oil temperature.

- Fry until the tempura is light golden and crispy, about 2-3 minutes for seafood and 1-2 minutes for vegetables. Avoid overcrowding the fryer to ensure even cooking.

4. Drain and Serve:

- Remove the cooked tempura with a slotted spoon or wire mesh skimmer, allowing excess oil to drip off.
- Transfer to a plate lined with paper towels to drain briefly.

5. Make Tempura Dipping Sauce (Tentsuyu):

- In a small saucepan, combine dashi (or water), soy sauce, mirin, and sugar. Bring to a simmer over medium heat, stirring until sugar is dissolved.
- Remove from heat and let cool. Optionally, add grated daikon radish or ginger to the sauce for extra flavor.

6. Serve Tempura:

- Arrange the cooked tempura on a serving plate. Serve immediately with tempura dipping sauce on the side.

Tips:

- **Temperature Control:** Maintain oil temperature around 340-350°F (170-180°C) for crispy tempura.
- **Batter Consistency:** The batter should be thin and cold for a light, crispy coating.
- **Variations:** Experiment with different seafood and vegetables to create a variety of tempura dishes.

Enjoy your homemade tempura with friends and family as a delightful appetizer or main course, paired with the flavorful dipping sauce!

Sukiyaki

Ingredients:

- **For Sukiyaki Sauce:**
    - 1 cup dashi (Japanese soup stock)
    - 1/2 cup soy sauce
    - 1/2 cup mirin (sweet rice wine)
    - 1/4 cup sugar
    - 2 tablespoons sake (Japanese rice wine)
- **For Sukiyaki Ingredients:**
    - 1 pound thinly sliced beef (preferably ribeye or sirloin)
    - 1/2 block of firm tofu, cut into cubes
    - 1 bunch of enoki mushrooms, bottom trimmed
    - 1/2 Napa cabbage, sliced into bite-sized pieces
    - 4-6 shiitake mushrooms, stems removed and sliced
    - 1 bunch of green onions, cut into 2-inch pieces
    - 1/2 package of shirataki noodles (optional), rinsed and drained
    - 1-2 tablespoons vegetable oil for cooking
- **For Serving:**
    - Cooked Japanese rice
    - Raw egg (optional, for dipping)

Instructions:

1. Prepare the Sukiyaki Sauce:

- In a small saucepan, combine dashi, soy sauce, mirin, sugar, and sake.
- Bring to a simmer over medium heat, stirring occasionally until sugar is dissolved.
- Reduce heat and keep warm while preparing the rest of the ingredients.

2. Prepare the Sukiyaki Ingredients:

- Heat a large skillet or a sukiyaki pan over medium heat. Add vegetable oil.
- Add thinly sliced beef to the skillet and cook until browned. Remove excess fat if necessary.
- Add tofu cubes, enoki mushrooms, shiitake mushrooms, Napa cabbage, and green onions to the skillet. Arrange them evenly around the skillet.

3. Cook Sukiyaki:

- Pour the prepared sukiyaki sauce over the ingredients in the skillet. Bring to a simmer.
- Allow the ingredients to cook in the simmering sauce for 5-7 minutes, or until vegetables are tender and beef is cooked through.

4. Serve Sukiyaki:

- Transfer the cooked sukiyaki to a serving bowl or keep it in the skillet if using a tabletop burner.
- Serve hot with cooked Japanese rice on the side.
- Optionally, crack a raw egg into a small bowl for each diner. Dip the cooked sukiyaki ingredients into the raw egg before eating for added richness and flavor.

Tips:

- **Dashi Substitute:** If you don't have dashi, you can use water or chicken broth as a substitute.
- **Vegetarian Option:** Substitute beef with tofu or additional mushrooms for a vegetarian version.
- **Tabletop Cooking:** Sukiyaki is often cooked at the table using a portable burner, allowing everyone to enjoy cooking and eating together.

Sukiyaki is a delightful dish that warms both the body and the soul, perfect for cold days or special gatherings. Enjoy the interactive and communal experience of cooking and eating sukiyaki with loved ones!

Shabu-Shabu

Ingredients:

- **For Shabu-Shabu Broth:**
    - 6 cups dashi (Japanese soup stock) or water
    - 1/4 cup soy sauce
    - 1/4 cup mirin (sweet rice wine)
    - 1 tablespoon sugar
    - 1/2 teaspoon salt
- **For Shabu-Shabu Ingredients:**
    - 1/2 pound thinly sliced beef (preferably ribeye or sirloin)
    - Assorted vegetables (napa cabbage, spinach, carrots, mushrooms, enoki mushrooms, tofu, etc.)
    - Shirataki noodles (optional)
    - 1 bunch of green onions, cut into 2-inch pieces
    - Shungiku (edible chrysanthemum leaves) or other leafy greens
    - 1 package of firm tofu, cubed
    - Cooked udon noodles (optional, for serving)
- **For Dipping Sauce (Ponzu):**
    - 1/2 cup soy sauce
    - 1/4 cup mirin (sweet rice wine)
    - 1/4 cup rice vinegar
    - 1 tablespoon lemon juice
    - 1 teaspoon sugar
    - 1/4 cup dashi (optional, for a lighter flavor)

Instructions:

1. Prepare Shabu-Shabu Broth:

- In a large pot or a shabu-shabu pot, combine dashi (or water), soy sauce, mirin, sugar, and salt.
- Bring the broth to a simmer over medium heat. Keep the broth simmering throughout the meal.

2. Prepare Shabu-Shabu Ingredients:

- Arrange thinly sliced beef, assorted vegetables, tofu, and shirataki noodles on a large serving platter or plate. Each diner should have their own plate of ingredients.

3. Cook Shabu-Shabu:

- Dip a slice of beef into the simmering broth and swish it back and forth (shabu-shabu motion) for a few seconds until it changes color and cooks to your desired doneness (usually just a few seconds for thin slices).
- Remove the beef from the broth and dip it into the ponzu dipping sauce (optional) before eating.
- Continue cooking and eating the beef and vegetables in batches, enjoying them with the dipping sauce or adding them directly into the broth to flavor it further.

4. Serve Shabu-Shabu:

- Serve hot with cooked udon noodles if desired.
- Enjoy the cooked ingredients with the ponzu dipping sauce or add additional seasoning to the broth as desired.

Tips:

- **Hot Pot Setup:** Use a portable gas burner or electric hot pot at the dining table for an authentic Shabu-Shabu experience.
- **Vegetarian Option:** Substitute thinly sliced tofu, mushrooms, and additional vegetables for the meat.
- **Enjoy the Process:** Shabu-Shabu is a communal meal where everyone cooks and eats together, enjoying the flavors of the simmering broth and fresh ingredients.

Shabu-Shabu is not only delicious but also a fun and interactive way to enjoy a meal with family and friends. Dive into this Japanese hot pot dish and savor the fresh flavors and tender meats!

Chirashi Sushi

Ingredients:

- **For Sushi Rice:**
    - 2 cups sushi rice
    - 2 cups water
    - 1/4 cup rice vinegar
    - 2 tablespoons sugar
    - 1 teaspoon salt
- **For Chirashi Toppings (Suggestions):**
    - Assorted sashimi (tuna, salmon, yellowtail, shrimp, etc.)
    - Sliced avocado
    - Cucumber, thinly sliced
    - Tamagoyaki (Japanese rolled omelette), sliced into strips
    - Crab sticks or real crab meat
    - Edamame beans
    - Pickled ginger (gari)
    - Nori (seaweed), thinly sliced
- **For Garnish:**
    - Sesame seeds (black or white)
    - Thinly sliced green onions (scallions)
- **For Serving:**
    - Soy sauce
    - Wasabi paste

Instructions:

1. Prepare Sushi Rice:

- Rinse the sushi rice in cold water until the water runs clear.
- Combine the rice and water in a rice cooker or pot. Cook according to the rice cooker's instructions or bring to a boil, then cover and simmer for 15-20 minutes until the water is absorbed.
- In a small saucepan, heat the rice vinegar, sugar, and salt over low heat until dissolved. Remove from heat.
- Transfer the cooked rice to a large bowl and gently fold in the vinegar mixture using a wooden spoon or rice paddle. Allow the rice to cool to room temperature.

2. Prepare Chirashi Toppings:

- Prepare the sashimi by slicing them thinly and arranging them on a plate or cutting board.
- Slice the avocado, cucumber, and tamagoyaki into thin strips or pieces.

- Prepare any other toppings you wish to include, such as crab sticks, edamame, pickled ginger, and nori strips.

3. Assemble Chirashi Sushi:

- Divide the sushi rice among serving bowls or a large serving platter.
- Arrange the assorted toppings over the sushi rice in an aesthetically pleasing manner. You can scatter them evenly or organize them in sections for a visually appealing presentation.
- Sprinkle sesame seeds and thinly sliced green onions over the toppings for garnish.

4. Serve Chirashi Sushi:

- Serve Chirashi Sushi with soy sauce and wasabi paste on the side.
- Optionally, provide pickled ginger (gari) as a palate cleanser between bites.

Tips:

- **Variety:** Chirashi Sushi allows for creativity with toppings. Use a combination of your favorite sashimi, vegetables, and other ingredients.
- **Presentation:** Arrange the toppings neatly and colorfully for an appetizing presentation.
- **Customization:** Customize the toppings based on personal preferences and seasonal availability of ingredients.

Chirashi Sushi is a delightful dish that showcases the freshness and flavors of Japanese cuisine. Enjoy this colorful and satisfying meal with friends and family!

Tonkatsu

Ingredients:

- **For Tonkatsu:**
    - 4 pork loin or pork tenderloin cutlets, about 1/2-inch thick
    - Salt and pepper
    - 1/2 cup all-purpose flour
    - 2 large eggs, beaten
    - 1 cup panko breadcrumbs (Japanese breadcrumbs)
    - Vegetable oil, for frying
- **For Serving:**
    - Tonkatsu sauce (or Worcestershire sauce mixed with ketchup)
    - Shredded cabbage
    - Cooked rice

Instructions:

1. Prepare the Pork Cutlets:

- Start by tenderizing the pork cutlets slightly with a meat mallet or the back of a knife to ensure even cooking.
- Season both sides of the pork cutlets with salt and pepper.

2. Breading Process:

- Set up a breading station with three shallow bowls or plates: one with flour, one with beaten eggs, and one with panko breadcrumbs.
- Dredge each pork cutlet in the flour, shaking off any excess.
- Dip the floured cutlets into the beaten eggs, coating them evenly.
- Press each cutlet firmly into the panko breadcrumbs, ensuring an even and thick coating. Gently pat the breadcrumbs onto the pork to help them adhere.

3. Fry the Tonkatsu:

- Heat vegetable oil in a deep frying pan or skillet to about 350°F (180°C) over medium heat. The oil should be enough to submerge the pork cutlets halfway.
- Carefully place the breaded pork cutlets into the hot oil, one or two at a time depending on the size of your pan. Fry for about 3-4 minutes on each side, or until golden brown and crispy.
- Remove the tonkatsu from the oil and drain on a wire rack or paper towels to remove excess oil.

4. Serve Tonkatsu:

- Slice the tonkatsu into strips or leave whole.
- Serve hot with shredded cabbage, tonkatsu sauce (or a mixture of Worcestershire sauce and ketchup), and steamed rice on the side.

Tips:

- **Panko Breadcrumbs:** Using panko breadcrumbs gives tonkatsu its characteristic crispy texture. Regular breadcrumbs can be used but won't provide the same crunch.
- **Oil Temperature:** Maintain a consistent oil temperature to ensure the tonkatsu cooks evenly and crisps up nicely without absorbing too much oil.
- **Serving Suggestions:** Tonkatsu is often served with shredded cabbage to add freshness and crunch, along with a tangy tonkatsu sauce for dipping.

Enjoy making this classic Japanese dish at home! Tonkatsu is satisfying and flavorful, perfect for a comforting meal any time of the year.

Okonomiyaki

Ingredients:

- **For Okonomiyaki Batter:**
    - 1 cup all-purpose flour
    - 1 cup dashi (Japanese soup stock) or water
    - 2 eggs
    - 1/2 small cabbage, finely shredded
    - 2 green onions, thinly sliced
    - 1/2 cup tenkasu (tempura crumbs) or panko breadcrumbs
    - Salt and pepper to taste
- **Optional Ingredients (choose one or more):**
    - Thinly sliced pork belly, shrimp, or squid
    - Thinly sliced vegetables (e.g., mushrooms, bell peppers)
    - Cooked noodles (yakisoba noodles work well)
    - Cheese, grated
- **For Toppings:**
    - Okonomiyaki sauce (or a mixture of 3 parts Worcestershire sauce and 1 part ketchup)
    - Japanese mayonnaise
    - Aonori (dried green seaweed flakes)
    - Katsuobushi (bonito flakes)

Instructions:

1. Prepare the Batter:

- In a large bowl, whisk together flour, dashi or water, and eggs until smooth.
- Add shredded cabbage, green onions, tenkasu or panko breadcrumbs, and any optional ingredients of your choice. Season with salt and pepper. Mix until everything is well combined.

2. Cook Okonomiyaki:

- Heat a large non-stick skillet or griddle over medium heat. Add a little vegetable oil and spread it around.
- Pour a portion of the batter onto the skillet to form a round pancake, about 6-8 inches in diameter and about 1/2 inch thick.
- If using thinly sliced pork belly or other meat, arrange it on top of the pancake.
- Cook for 4-5 minutes, or until the bottom is golden brown and crispy.
- Carefully flip the okonomiyaki using a spatula and cook the other side for another 4-5 minutes, or until golden brown and cooked through.

3. Serve Okonomiyaki:

- Transfer the cooked okonomiyaki to a serving plate.
- Drizzle okonomiyaki sauce and Japanese mayonnaise over the top in a crisscross pattern.
- Sprinkle with aonori (dried seaweed flakes) and katsuobushi (bonito flakes) for extra flavor and texture.

4. Enjoy:

- Cut the okonomiyaki into wedges and serve immediately while hot.
- Okonomiyaki is often enjoyed as a main dish or appetizer, and it's common to eat it with chopsticks or a fork.

Tips:

- **Customization:** Feel free to customize your okonomiyaki with your favorite ingredients. The recipe is very versatile!
- **Cooking:** Make sure the okonomiyaki is cooked through and crispy on both sides for the best texture.
- **Serving:** Okonomiyaki is often served as a communal dish, where everyone can cut their own piece and enjoy the toppings.

Okonomiyaki is not only delicious but also fun to make and customize according to your preferences. Enjoy this iconic Japanese dish at home with friends and family!

Yakitori

Ingredients:

- **For Yakitori:**
    - 1 lb chicken thighs or chicken breast, cut into bite-sized pieces
    - Bamboo skewers (if using wooden skewers, soak them in water for 30 minutes to prevent burning)
    - Salt and pepper
    - Optional: green onions, bell peppers, mushrooms (for additional skewers)
- **For Yakitori Sauce (Tare):**
    - 1/2 cup soy sauce
    - 1/2 cup mirin (sweet rice wine)
    - 1/4 cup sake (Japanese rice wine)
    - 2 tablespoons sugar
    - 1 clove garlic, grated (optional)
    - 1 teaspoon grated ginger (optional)
- **For Serving (Optional):**
    - Shichimi togarashi (Japanese seven-spice blend)
    - Lemon wedges

Instructions:

1. Prepare Yakitori Sauce (Tare):

- In a small saucepan, combine soy sauce, mirin, sake, sugar, garlic (if using), and ginger (if using).
- Bring the mixture to a boil over medium heat, then reduce the heat to low.
- Simmer for 10-15 minutes, stirring occasionally, until the sauce is slightly thickened. Remove from heat and set aside to cool.

2. Prepare Chicken Skewers:

- Season the chicken pieces with salt and pepper.
- Thread the chicken onto skewers, alternating with pieces of green onions, bell peppers, or mushrooms if desired. Leave a little space between each piece for even cooking.

3. Grill Yakitori:

- Preheat your grill (charcoal or gas) to medium-high heat.
- Brush the grill grates with oil to prevent sticking.
- Place the chicken skewers on the grill and cook for about 3-4 minutes per side, or until the chicken is cooked through and nicely charred.
- While grilling, baste the skewers with the yakitori sauce (tare) using a brush, turning them occasionally and basting until they are fully coated and caramelized.

4. Serve Yakitori:

- Remove the cooked yakitori skewers from the grill and place them on a serving platter.
- Optionally, sprinkle with shichimi togarashi (Japanese seven-spice blend) for added flavor and spice.
- Serve hot with lemon wedges on the side for squeezing over the yakitori.

Tips:

- **Variations:** Yakitori can be made with various cuts of chicken, and you can also use different vegetables or even seafood.
- **Grilling:** Keep an eye on the skewers while grilling to prevent burning. Adjust the heat if necessary.
- **Serving:** Yakitori is often served as an appetizer or as part of a meal with rice and other side dishes.

Yakitori is a delicious and savory dish that's perfect for grilling outdoors or even indoors using a grill pan. Enjoy making and eating yakitori with friends and family!

Miso Soup with Clams

Ingredients:

- **For Miso Soup:**
    - 4 cups dashi (Japanese soup stock) or water
    - 1/4 cup miso paste (white or red, according to preference)
    - 1/2 block tofu, cut into small cubes
    - 1 cup fresh clams (asari clams), cleaned and scrubbed
    - 2 green onions, thinly sliced
    - 1 sheet of nori (seaweed), cut into thin strips (optional)
    - 1 tablespoon soy sauce (optional, for seasoning)
- **For Garnish (Optional):**
    - Thinly sliced green onions
    - Seaweed flakes (aonori) or toasted sesame seeds

Instructions:

1. Prepare the Clams:

- Rinse the clams thoroughly under cold water, scrubbing off any dirt or debris. Soak them in salted water for about 30 minutes to help remove any sand or grit. Drain and rinse again.

2. Make the Miso Soup Base:

- In a medium pot, bring dashi or water to a simmer over medium heat.
- Add tofu cubes and simmer for 2-3 minutes until tofu is heated through.

3. Add Clams to the Soup:

- Carefully add the cleaned clams to the pot.
- Cook for about 3-5 minutes, or until the clams open up. Discard any clams that do not open.

4. Prepare Miso Paste:

- In a small bowl, whisk together miso paste with a ladleful of hot soup broth until smooth.

5. Finish the Miso Soup:

- Reduce heat to low. Add the miso paste mixture to the pot, stirring gently to combine. Be careful not to boil the miso, as it can lose its flavor.
- Taste and adjust seasoning with soy sauce if desired, although the broth from the clams may already provide enough saltiness.

6. Serve Miso Soup:

- Ladle the miso soup with clams and tofu into serving bowls.
- Garnish with thinly sliced green onions, nori strips (if using), and a sprinkle of seaweed flakes or toasted sesame seeds for added flavor and texture.

Tips:

- **Dashi Substitute:** If you don't have dashi, you can use water or a combination of water and instant dashi granules or dashi powder.
- **Miso Paste:** Adjust the amount of miso paste according to your preference for saltiness and depth of flavor.
- **Clam Handling:** Be sure to discard any clams that do not open after cooking, as they may not be safe to eat.

Asari miso soup with clams is a delicious and nourishing dish, perfect as a starter or part of a Japanese meal. Enjoy its umami-rich flavor and comforting warmth!

Udon Noodles with Tempura

Ingredients:

- **For Udon Noodles:**
    - 4 portions of fresh or dried udon noodles
    - 6 cups dashi (Japanese soup stock) or water
    - 1/4 cup soy sauce
    - 2 tablespoons mirin (sweet rice wine)
    - 2 tablespoons sake (Japanese rice wine) (optional)
    - 1 tablespoon sugar
    - 2 cups fresh spinach leaves, washed
    - 4 green onions, thinly sliced
    - 4 sheets of nori (seaweed), cut into thin strips (optional)
    - Shichimi togarashi (Japanese seven-spice blend) for garnish (optional)
- **For Tempura:**
    - Assorted vegetables and seafood (shrimp, sweet potato, zucchini, mushrooms, etc.)
    - 1 cup all-purpose flour
    - 1/2 cup cornstarch
    - 1 teaspoon baking powder
    - 1 cup ice-cold water
    - Ice cubes
    - Oil for deep frying (vegetable oil or canola oil)

Instructions:

1. Prepare Udon Noodles:

- Cook udon noodles according to package instructions. Drain and rinse under cold water to remove excess starch.

2. Make Udon Broth:

- In a medium pot, combine dashi (or water), soy sauce, mirin, sake (if using), and sugar. Bring to a simmer over medium heat.
- Add fresh spinach leaves and cook for 1-2 minutes until wilted.
- Remove from heat and keep warm.

3. Prepare Tempura:

- Heat oil in a deep fryer or large pot to 340-350°F (170-180°C).
- In a large bowl, sift together flour, cornstarch, and baking powder.
- Gradually add ice-cold water to the flour mixture, whisking gently until just combined. The batter should be slightly lumpy and thinner than pancake batter.

- Place a few ice cubes in the batter to keep it cold, which helps create a crispy texture.
- Dip each piece of seafood or vegetable into the tempura batter, allowing excess batter to drip off.
- Carefully place battered pieces into the hot oil, frying a few pieces at a time to maintain oil temperature. Fry until light golden and crispy, about 2-3 minutes for seafood and 1-2 minutes for vegetables. Avoid overcrowding the fryer to ensure even cooking.
- Remove tempura with a slotted spoon or wire mesh skimmer and drain on a plate lined with paper towels.

4. Serve Udon Noodles with Tempura:

- Divide cooked udon noodles into serving bowls.
- Ladle hot udon broth with spinach over the noodles.
- Arrange tempura on top of the noodles or serve on the side.
- Garnish with sliced green onions, nori strips (if using), and a sprinkle of shichimi togarashi for added flavor and spice.

Tips:

- **Variations:** Feel free to customize your tempura with your favorite vegetables and seafood.
- **Temperature Control:** Maintain oil temperature around 340-350°F (170-180°C) for crispy tempura.
- **Presentation:** Serve udon noodles and tempura separately if you prefer to maintain crispiness.

Udon noodles with tempura is a delicious and satisfying dish that combines the textures of chewy noodles and crispy tempura with a flavorful broth. Enjoy this comforting Japanese meal at home!

Teriyaki Chicken

Ingredients:

- **For Teriyaki Sauce:**
    - 1/2 cup soy sauce
    - 1/4 cup mirin (sweet rice wine)
    - 1/4 cup sake (Japanese rice wine) or dry white wine
    - 3 tablespoons sugar
    - 2 cloves garlic, minced
    - 1 teaspoon grated ginger (optional)
    - 1 tablespoon cornstarch mixed with 2 tablespoons water (optional, for thickening)
- **For Chicken:**
    - 4 boneless, skinless chicken thighs or chicken breasts
    - Salt and pepper
    - 2 tablespoons vegetable oil
- **For Garnish (Optional):**
    - Sesame seeds
    - Thinly sliced green onions
    - Steamed rice or vegetables for serving

Instructions:

1. Prepare Teriyaki Sauce:

- In a small saucepan, combine soy sauce, mirin, sake (or white wine), sugar, minced garlic, and grated ginger (if using).
- Bring the mixture to a boil over medium heat, then reduce the heat to low and simmer for 8-10 minutes, stirring occasionally, until the sauce thickens slightly.
- If you prefer a thicker sauce, stir in the cornstarch mixture and cook for another 1-2 minutes until the sauce reaches your desired consistency. Remove from heat and set aside.

2. Prepare Chicken:

- Season both sides of the chicken thighs or breasts with salt and pepper.
- Heat vegetable oil in a large skillet or grill pan over medium-high heat.
- Add the chicken to the skillet and cook for 6-7 minutes per side, or until the chicken is cooked through and golden brown on the outside. Cooking time will vary depending on the thickness of the chicken pieces.
- If using a meat thermometer, the internal temperature should reach 165°F (75°C) for chicken to be fully cooked.

3. Glaze with Teriyaki Sauce:

- Once the chicken is cooked, reduce the heat to low and pour the prepared teriyaki sauce over the chicken in the skillet.
- Turn the chicken pieces to coat evenly in the sauce. Allow the chicken to simmer in the sauce for 1-2 minutes to absorb the flavors and thicken the sauce slightly.

4. Serve Teriyaki Chicken:

- Transfer the teriyaki chicken to a serving platter or individual plates.
- Garnish with sesame seeds and thinly sliced green onions.
- Serve hot with steamed rice or vegetables on the side.

Tips:

- **Marinating:** For extra flavor, you can marinate the chicken in a portion of the teriyaki sauce for 30 minutes to 1 hour before cooking.
- **Grilling Option:** Teriyaki chicken can also be grilled. Preheat the grill to medium-high heat and grill the chicken until cooked through, then brush with the teriyaki sauce during the last few minutes of cooking.
- **Sauce Variations:** Adjust the sweetness or saltiness of the teriyaki sauce according to your taste preference by adjusting the amount of sugar or soy sauce.

Teriyaki chicken is a delicious and versatile dish that pairs well with rice or vegetables. Enjoy making this flavorful Japanese dish at home!

Grilled Mackerel with Miso

Ingredients:

- **For Grilled Mackerel:**
    - 4 mackerel fillets (saba), about 6-8 ounces each
    - Salt
    - Vegetable oil (for brushing)
- **For Miso Glaze:**
    - 1/4 cup white miso paste
    - 2 tablespoons mirin (sweet rice wine)
    - 1 tablespoon sake (Japanese rice wine) or dry white wine
    - 1 tablespoon sugar
- **For Garnish:**
    - Thinly sliced green onions
    - Toasted sesame seeds

Instructions:

1. Prepare Miso Glaze:

- In a small saucepan, combine white miso paste, mirin, sake (or white wine), and sugar.
- Cook over low heat, stirring constantly, until the miso paste is dissolved and the mixture is smooth. Remove from heat and set aside to cool slightly.

2. Prepare Mackerel Fillets:

- Pat the mackerel fillets dry with paper towels.
- Lightly score the skin side of each fillet with a knife. This helps the fish cook evenly and allows the flavors to penetrate.

3. Grill Mackerel:

- Preheat the grill to medium-high heat.
- Brush both sides of the mackerel fillets lightly with vegetable oil and season with a little salt.
- Place the fillets on the grill, skin side down first. Grill for about 3-4 minutes per side, or until the skin is crispy and the flesh is cooked through. Cooking time will depend on the thickness of the fillets.
- Alternatively, you can broil the mackerel fillets in the oven. Preheat the broiler and place the fillets on a lined baking sheet. Broil for 5-7 minutes, or until the fish is cooked through and lightly browned.

4. Glaze with Miso Sauce:

- Brush the cooked mackerel fillets generously with the prepared miso glaze on both sides.
- Return the fillets to the grill or broiler for another 1-2 minutes, or until the miso glaze is caramelized and bubbly. Watch closely to prevent burning.

5. Serve Grilled Mackerel with Miso:

- Transfer the grilled mackerel fillets to a serving platter.
- Garnish with thinly sliced green onions and toasted sesame seeds.
- Serve hot with steamed rice and your favorite vegetables or a side salad.

Tips:

- **Variation:** You can also pan-fry the mackerel fillets instead of grilling them.
- **Marinating:** For extra flavor, you can marinate the mackerel fillets in a portion of the miso glaze for 30 minutes to 1 hour before grilling.
- **Serving Suggestions:** Grilled mackerel with miso is typically served as a main dish in a traditional Japanese meal. It pairs wonderfully with steamed rice and a side of pickled vegetables or a light salad.

Enjoy making this delicious and flavorful Grilled Mackerel with Miso dish at home!

Kaiseki Ryori (Traditional Multi-course Meal)

Menu Overview:

1. **Sakizuke (Appetizers)**
   - Assorted Sashimi Appetizer
2. **Suimono (Soup)**
   - Clear Soup with Tofu and Wakame
3. **Mukozuke (Sashimi)**
   - Sashimi Platter with Soy Sauce, Wasabi, and Daikon
4. **Yakimono (Grilled Dish)**
   - Miso-Marinated Black Cod (Gindara)
5. **Nimono (Simmered Dish)**
   - Simmered Vegetables in Dashi Broth
6. **Agemono (Deep-fried Dish)**
   - Tempura Assortment (Shrimp, Sweet Potato, Shiitake)
7. **Sunomono (Vinegared Dish)**
   - Assorted Pickles (Tsukemono)
8. **Shokuji (Rice Dish)**
   - Steamed Rice with Miso Soup (Tofu and Wakame)
9. **Mizumono (Dessert)**
   - Seasonal Fruit Platter

Detailed Preparation:

1. Sakizuke (Appetizers):

- **Assorted Sashimi Appetizer:**
  - Arrange slices of fresh sashimi (tuna, salmon, yellowtail) on a plate.
  - Garnish with daikon radish, shiso leaves, and lemon slices.

2. Suimono (Soup):

- **Clear Soup with Tofu and Wakame:**
  - Prepare dashi broth using dashi kombu and bonito flakes.
  - Add tofu cubes and wakame seaweed.
  - Season lightly with soy sauce and garnish with thinly sliced green onions.

3. Mukozuke (Sashimi):

- **Sashimi Platter with Condiments:**
  - Arrange fresh sashimi slices on a serving platter.
  - Serve with soy sauce, wasabi, and grated daikon radish.

4. Yakimono (Grilled Dish):

- **Miso-Marinated Black Cod (Gindara):**
  - Marinate black cod fillets in a mixture of white miso paste, mirin, and sake.
  - Grill until the fish is cooked through and caramelized. Serve with a wedge of lemon.

5. Nimono (Simmered Dish):

- **Simmered Vegetables in Dashi Broth:**
  - Prepare seasonal vegetables (carrots, lotus root, bamboo shoots) in dashi broth.
  - Season with soy sauce, mirin, and sugar until tender and flavorful.

6. Agemono (Deep-fried Dish):

- **Tempura Assortment (Shrimp, Sweet Potato, Shiitake):**
  - Prepare tempura batter with a mixture of flour, cornstarch, and ice-cold water.
  - Dip shrimp, sweet potato slices, and shiitake mushrooms in the batter and deep-fry until crispy.
  - Serve with tempura dipping sauce.

7. Sunomono (Vinegared Dish):

- **Assorted Pickles (Tsukemono):**
  - Serve a selection of pickled vegetables (cucumber, radish, eggplant) in a vinegar-based dressing.

8. Shokuji (Rice Dish):

- **Steamed Rice with Miso Soup (Tofu and Wakame):**
  - Cook short-grain Japanese rice and serve in individual bowls.
  - Prepare miso soup with tofu cubes and wakame seaweed.

9. Mizumono (Dessert):

- **Seasonal Fruit Platter:**
  - Arrange a selection of fresh seasonal fruits (melon, grapes, strawberries) on a platter.
  - Serve with green tea or a light sweet syrup.

Serving Tips:

- **Presentation:** Arrange each dish carefully, paying attention to aesthetics and balance.

- **Sequence:** Serve each course in the traditional order, ensuring that flavors and textures complement each other.
- **Enjoyment:** Encourage guests to savor each course slowly, appreciating the variety and **craftsmanship of each dish.**

Oden (Japanese Hot Pot)

Ingredients:

- **For Dashi Broth:**
    - 8 cups water
    - 2 pieces kombu (dried kelp), each about 4 inches long
    - 1 cup bonito flakes (katsuobushi)
- **For Oden Ingredients (Customizable):**
    - 4 hard-boiled eggs, peeled
    - 4 Japanese daikon radishes, peeled and cut into thick rounds
    - 4-6 pieces konnyaku (yam cake), cut into bite-sized pieces
    - 4-6 pieces aburaage (fried tofu pouches), cut in half
    - 4-6 pieces ganmodoki (tofu and vegetable fritters), optional
    - 4-6 pieces chikuwa (tube-shaped fish cake), sliced diagonally
    - 4-6 pieces hanpen (fish cake made from ground fish), optional
    - 4-6 pieces boiled potatoes, peeled and halved
    - 4-6 pieces boiled eggs, peeled and halved
    - Mustard (for serving)
    - Soy sauce (for serving)
    - Grated daikon radish (for serving)
    - Chopped green onions (for garnish)

Instructions:

1. Prepare Dashi Broth:

- In a large pot, combine water and kombu. Let it sit for 30 minutes to allow the kombu to release its flavor.
- Place the pot over medium heat and slowly bring to a simmer. Just before it starts to boil, remove the kombu.
- Add bonito flakes to the pot, bring it to a boil, then reduce the heat and simmer for 5 minutes.
- Remove the pot from heat and let the bonito flakes sink to the bottom.
- Strain the dashi through a fine sieve or cheesecloth. Set aside.

2. Prepare Oden Ingredients:

- Prepare the hard-boiled eggs and peeled potatoes if not already done.
- Cut daikon radishes into thick rounds and score each round with a crisscross pattern to help absorb flavors.
- Cut konnyaku into bite-sized pieces and score them as well to absorb flavors.

3. Cook Oden:

- Return the strained dashi broth to a clean pot.
- Add daikon radish, konnyaku, aburaage, ganmodoki, chikuwa, hanpen, boiled potatoes, and boiled eggs to the pot.
- Bring the broth to a simmer over medium heat.

4. Simmer Oden:

- Once simmering, reduce heat to low and cover the pot. Let it simmer gently for about 1-1.5 hours, or until the daikon radish is tender and infused with flavor.
- Occasionally skim any foam that rises to the surface.

5. Serve Oden:

- To serve, place assorted Oden ingredients into bowls or deep plates.
- Serve with mustard and soy sauce on the side for dipping.
- Optionally, offer grated daikon radish as a topping.
- Garnish with chopped green onions for added flavor and color.

Tips:

- **Customize Ingredients:** Feel free to add or substitute Oden ingredients based on your preferences. Some common additions include fish cakes, fish balls, tofu, or other vegetables.
- **Flavor Enhancements:** Adjust the seasoning by adding soy sauce or mirin to the broth if desired.
- **Serving Style:** Oden is often enjoyed as a communal dish where diners can choose their favorite ingredients from the simmering pot.

Oden is a comforting and versatile dish that allows for creativity in ingredient selection while providing a warming meal perfect for chilly evenings. Enjoy the process of simmering and the delightful flavors of this traditional Japanese hot pot!

Yakiniku (Japanese BBQ)

Ingredients:

- **For Yakiniku Marinade:**
    - 1/2 cup soy sauce
    - 1/4 cup sake (Japanese rice wine)
    - 2 tablespoons mirin (sweet rice wine)
    - 2 tablespoons sugar
    - 2 cloves garlic, minced
    - 1 teaspoon grated ginger
    - 1 tablespoon sesame oil (optional, for extra flavor)
- **For Yakiniku Meat:**
    - 1 pound thinly sliced beef (such as ribeye, sirloin, or skirt steak)
    - 1 pound thinly sliced pork (such as pork belly or loin)
    - Assorted vegetables (such as bell peppers, mushrooms, zucchini) for grilling
- **For Serving:**
    - Steamed rice
    - Lettuce leaves (for wrapping)
    - Yakiniku dipping sauce (tare sauce)
    - Sesame seeds (for garnish)
    - Thinly sliced green onions (for garnish)

Instructions:

1. Prepare Yakiniku Marinade:

- In a bowl, whisk together soy sauce, sake, mirin, sugar, minced garlic, grated ginger, and sesame oil (if using) until the sugar is dissolved.
- Reserve about 1/4 cup of the marinade for basting and serving.

2. Marinate the Meat:

- Place the thinly sliced beef and pork in separate bowls.
- Pour the marinade over the meat, ensuring it is evenly coated. Cover and refrigerate for at least 30 minutes to marinate. You can marinate for longer (up to 2 hours) for more flavor.

3. Prepare Vegetables:

- Cut assorted vegetables into bite-sized pieces suitable for grilling, such as bell peppers, mushrooms, and zucchini.
- If using wooden skewers for vegetables, soak them in water for at least 30 minutes to prevent burning.

4. Heat the Grill:

- Preheat a grill pan, outdoor grill, or tabletop electric grill to medium-high heat.
- Brush the grill lightly with oil to prevent sticking.

5. Grill the Meat and Vegetables:

- Remove the marinated meat from the marinade and shake off excess liquid.
- Grill the meat and vegetables in batches, turning occasionally, until cooked through and lightly charred on the edges. Cooking time will vary depending on the thickness of the meat slices.
- Use the reserved marinade to baste the meat while grilling for added flavor.

6. Serve Yakiniku:

- Transfer grilled meat and vegetables to a serving platter.
- Sprinkle with sesame seeds and thinly sliced green onions for garnish.
- Serve with steamed rice, lettuce leaves for wrapping, and Yakiniku dipping sauce (tare sauce) on the side.
- To eat, place a piece of grilled meat and/or vegetables on a lettuce leaf, add a small amount of rice and a drizzle of dipping sauce, wrap, and enjoy!

Tips:

- **Grilling Options:** Yakiniku can be cooked on a traditional charcoal grill, a gas grill, or an indoor grill pan. The key is to get a good sear while maintaining the juiciness of the meat.
- **Dipping Sauce:** Yakiniku dipping sauce (tare sauce) can be adjusted to your taste with additional soy sauce, mirin, or sugar.
- **Variety:** Explore different cuts of meat and vegetables for a variety of flavors and textures.

Yakiniku is a delightful and interactive dining experience that brings friends and family together to enjoy grilled meats and vegetables with savory dipping sauce. Customize your Yakiniku with your favorite ingredients and enjoy the flavors of this Japanese barbecue at home!

Chawanmushi (Steamed Egg Custard)

Ingredients:

- **For the Custard Base:**
    - 2 cups dashi stock (Japanese soup stock)
    - 4 large eggs
    - 1 tablespoon soy sauce
    - 1 tablespoon mirin (sweet rice wine)
    - 1/2 teaspoon salt
    - 1/2 teaspoon sugar
- **For Filling (Customizable, choose a combination):**
    - 4 medium shrimp, peeled and deveined
    - 4 shiitake mushrooms, stems removed and thinly sliced
    - 1/2 cup diced chicken breast or thigh
    - 4 slices kamaboko (Japanese fish cake)
    - 4 pieces ginkgo nuts (optional)
    - 2-3 stalks mitsuba (Japanese parsley) or thinly sliced green onions for garnish

Instructions:

1. Prepare Dashi Stock:

- In a saucepan, bring dashi stock to a simmer over medium heat. If using instant dashi powder, follow package instructions to prepare.

2. Prepare Custard Base:

- In a mixing bowl, lightly beat eggs.
- Gradually add warm dashi stock to the eggs while whisking gently.
- Stir in soy sauce, mirin, salt, and sugar until well combined. Strain the mixture through a fine sieve to ensure a smooth custard base.

3. Prepare Filling Ingredients:

- Divide the filling ingredients (shrimp, mushrooms, chicken, kamaboko, ginkgo nuts) evenly among 4 Chawanmushi cups or small heatproof bowls.

4. Pour Custard Mixture:

- Carefully pour the custard mixture over the filling ingredients in each cup or bowl, leaving a little space at the top for the custard to expand during steaming.

5. Steam Chawanmushi:

- Prepare a steamer with enough water and bring it to a simmer.

- Place the Chawanmushi cups or bowls in the steamer, cover with a lid, and steam over medium-low heat for about 15-20 minutes, or until the custard is set. To check doneness, insert a toothpick into the custard; it should come out clean when done.

6. Serve Chawanmushi:

- Carefully remove the Chawanmushi cups or bowls from the steamer.
- Garnish each custard with mitsuba or thinly sliced green onions.
- Serve hot as an appetizer or side dish. It can be enjoyed on its own or with a side of soy sauce for dipping.

Tips:

- **Customization:** Feel free to customize the filling ingredients based on your preference or what's available. Traditional choices include seafood like shrimp and mushrooms, but you can also add ingredients like tofu, crab meat, or vegetables.
- **Steaming:** Ensure the steamer is not boiling vigorously to avoid overcooking the custard. Gentle steaming results in a silky-smooth texture.
- **Presentation:** Serve Chawanmushi in the cups or bowls they were steamed in to preserve their delicate appearance.

Chawanmushi is a wonderful dish that showcases the delicate flavors of Japanese cuisine and is perfect for a cozy meal or as part of a larger Japanese-themed dinner. Enjoy making and savoring this traditional Japanese steamed egg custard at home!

Takoyaki (Octopus Balls)

Ingredients:

- **For the Batter:**
    - 1 cup all-purpose flour
    - 1 1/2 cups dashi stock (Japanese soup stock)
    - 2 large eggs
    - 1/2 teaspoon salt
    - 1/2 teaspoon sugar
    - 1 tablespoon soy sauce
    - 1 tablespoon mirin (sweet rice wine)
- **For Filling:**
    - 1 cup diced cooked octopus (about 1 small octopus)
    - 1/4 cup chopped pickled ginger (beni shoga)
    - 1/4 cup chopped green onions
    - Optional: tempura scraps (tenkasu), bonito flakes (katsuobushi), and nori seaweed flakes for topping
- **For Cooking:**
    - Takoyaki pan (specialized pan with half-spherical molds)
    - Vegetable oil for greasing and cooking
    - Takoyaki pick or skewer (for turning)
- **For Garnish (Optional):**
    - Takoyaki sauce (or tonkatsu sauce)
    - Japanese mayonnaise
    - Aonori (dried seaweed flakes)
    - Katsuobushi (bonito flakes)

Instructions:

1. Prepare Takoyaki Batter:

- In a large bowl, whisk together flour, dashi stock, eggs, salt, sugar, soy sauce, and mirin until smooth. The batter should be thin and pourable.

2. Prepare Filling:

- Dice the cooked octopus into small pieces.
- Chop pickled ginger and green onions into small pieces.
- Combine octopus, pickled ginger, and green onions in a bowl.

3. Heat Takoyaki Pan:

- Preheat the takoyaki pan over medium heat.
- Brush each mold with vegetable oil to prevent sticking.

4. Cook Takoyaki:

- Pour batter into each mold until nearly full.
- Add a spoonful of octopus filling into each mold.
- As the batter begins to cook and set around the edges, use a takoyaki pick or skewer to gradually rotate the ball in the mold, allowing the uncooked batter to flow into the gaps. Continue rotating until the balls are evenly round and golden brown.
- Cook for about 3-4 minutes, rotating frequently, until the surface is crisp and golden and the inside is cooked through.

5. Serve Takoyaki:

- Remove takoyaki from the pan and place them on a plate.
- Drizzle with takoyaki sauce (or tonkatsu sauce) and Japanese mayonnaise.
- Sprinkle with aonori (seaweed flakes) and katsuobushi (bonito flakes).
- Serve hot, ideally with toothpicks or skewers for easy handling.

Tips:

- **Handling the Pan:** Takoyaki requires some practice to get the flipping technique right. Rotate the balls in the mold gradually to ensure even cooking and a round shape.
- **Customization:** Feel free to adjust the filling ingredients based on your preference. Some variations include cheese, kimchi, or other seafood.
- **Topping Options:** Experiment with different toppings such as chili powder, sesame seeds, or even a squeeze of lemon for a unique flavor twist.

Takoyaki is best enjoyed fresh and hot off the pan, capturing the delicious combination of tender octopus, savory batter, and flavorful toppings. It's a fun and delicious dish to make at home for a taste of Japanese street food culture!

Gyoza (Japanese Dumplings)

Ingredients:

- **For the Gyoza Wrappers:**
  - 25-30 round gyoza wrappers (store-bought or homemade)
- **For the Filling:**
  - 1/2 pound ground pork
  - 1 cup cabbage, finely chopped
  - 2-3 green onions, finely chopped
  - 2 cloves garlic, minced
  - 1 teaspoon ginger, grated
  - 1 tablespoon soy sauce
  - 1 tablespoon sake (Japanese rice wine) or mirin (sweet rice wine)
  - 1 teaspoon sesame oil
  - 1/2 teaspoon sugar
  - 1/4 teaspoon salt
  - 1/4 teaspoon pepper
- **For Cooking:**
  - 2 tablespoons vegetable oil, divided
  - 1/2 cup water
- **For Dipping Sauce:**
  - 2 tablespoons soy sauce
  - 1 tablespoon rice vinegar
  - 1/2 teaspoon sesame oil
  - Optional: chili oil or rayu (Japanese chili oil), for extra spice

Instructions:

1. Prepare the Filling:

- In a large bowl, combine ground pork, chopped cabbage, green onions, minced garlic, grated ginger, soy sauce, sake or mirin, sesame oil, sugar, salt, and pepper. Mix well until evenly combined.

2. Assemble the Gyoza:

- Place a gyoza wrapper on a clean surface.
- Spoon about 1 tablespoon of filling into the center of the wrapper.
- Moisten the edge of the wrapper with water using your fingertip.
- Fold the wrapper in half over the filling to create a half-moon shape. Pinch the edges together to seal, pleating one side if desired. Repeat with remaining wrappers and filling.

3. Cook the Gyoza:

- Heat 1 tablespoon of vegetable oil in a large non-stick skillet over medium-high heat.
- Arrange the gyoza in a single layer in the skillet, flat side down. Cook for 2-3 minutes or until the bottoms are golden brown.

4. Steam the Gyoza:

- Carefully pour 1/2 cup of water into the skillet. Immediately cover with a lid to steam the gyoza.
- Reduce the heat to medium-low and steam for about 5-7 minutes, or until the water has evaporated and the filling is cooked through.

5. Crisp the Bottoms:

- Remove the lid and increase the heat to medium-high. Cook for an additional 1-2 minutes, or until the bottoms of the gyoza are crispy and golden brown.

6. Make the Dipping Sauce:

- While the gyoza are cooking, prepare the dipping sauce by combining soy sauce, rice vinegar, and sesame oil in a small bowl. Add chili oil or rayu for extra spice if desired.

7. Serve Gyoza:

- Transfer the cooked gyoza to a serving plate, crispy side down.
- Serve immediately with the dipping sauce on the side.

Tips:

- **Freezing Gyoza:** If making ahead, freeze uncooked gyoza in a single layer on a baking sheet. Once frozen, transfer to a freezer bag for storage. Cook from frozen, adding extra cooking time.
- **Variations:** Experiment with different fillings such as shrimp and garlic chives or vegetarian options with tofu and shiitake mushrooms.
- **Dipping Sauce:** Adjust the dipping sauce to your taste by adding more vinegar for tanginess or more sesame oil for richness.

Gyoza are versatile and make for a delicious appetizer or main dish. Enjoy these homemade Japanese dumplings with family and friends, and savor the crispy exterior and juicy filling!

Unagi Don (Grilled Eel Rice Bowl)

Ingredients:

- **For the Unagi Don:**
    - 2 unagi fillets (fresh or pre-cooked, depending on availability)
    - 2 cups steamed Japanese rice
- **For the Sauce:**
    - 1/4 cup soy sauce
    - 1/4 cup mirin (sweet rice wine)
    - 2 tablespoons sugar
    - 2 tablespoons sake (Japanese rice wine)
    - 1 teaspoon cornstarch mixed with 1 tablespoon water (optional, for thickening)
- **Optional Toppings:**
    - Toasted sesame seeds
    - Sliced nori (seaweed)
    - Pickled ginger (gari)

Instructions:

1. Prepare the Sauce:

- In a small saucepan, combine soy sauce, mirin, sugar, and sake.
- Bring to a simmer over medium heat, stirring occasionally, until the sugar dissolves.
- If you prefer a thicker sauce, add the cornstarch mixture and stir until the sauce thickens slightly. Remove from heat and set aside.

2. Prepare the Unagi:

- If using fresh unagi fillets, preheat the grill or broiler. Score the skin side of the unagi fillets diagonally.
- Grill or broil the unagi fillets for about 3-4 minutes on each side, or until the skin is crispy and the flesh is heated through. If using pre-cooked unagi, skip this step.

3. Assemble Unagi Don:

- Divide the steamed rice into serving bowls.
- Place the grilled or pre-cooked unagi fillets on top of the rice.
- Drizzle the prepared sauce generously over the unagi and rice.

4. Garnish and Serve:

- Sprinkle toasted sesame seeds over the Unagi Don.
- Optionally, garnish with sliced nori and serve with pickled ginger on the side.

5. Enjoy:

- Serve Unagi Don immediately while warm, allowing the flavors to meld together.

Tips:

- **Grilling Unagi:** If grilling fresh unagi fillets, ensure the grill or broiler is well-heated to achieve a crispy skin and tender flesh.
- **Sauce Consistency:** Adjust the thickness of the sauce to your preference by adding more or less cornstarch slurry.
- **Rice:** Use Japanese short-grain rice for an authentic texture and taste. Rinse the rice well before cooking to remove excess starch.
- **Leftovers:** Unagi Don is best enjoyed fresh, but leftovers can be refrigerated and reheated gently in the microwave or steamed to preserve flavors.

Unagi Don is a satisfying dish that balances the sweetness of the sauce with the rich flavor of grilled eel, perfect for a special meal at home. Enjoy this traditional Japanese delicacy with its comforting flavors!

Katsudon (Pork Cutlet Rice Bowl)

Ingredients:

- **For the Pork Cutlets (Tonkatsu):**
    - 4 pork loin cutlets, about 1/2 inch thick
    - Salt and pepper
    - All-purpose flour, for dredging
    - 1-2 eggs, beaten
    - Panko breadcrumbs, for coating
    - Vegetable oil, for frying
- **For the Katsudon Sauce:**
    - 1 cup dashi stock (or substitute with chicken or vegetable broth)
    - 2 tablespoons soy sauce
    - 2 tablespoons mirin (sweet rice wine)
    - 1 tablespoon sugar
    - 1 onion, thinly sliced
- **For Assembly:**
    - Steamed Japanese rice
    - 4 eggs, lightly beaten
    - Chopped green onions, for garnish
    - Pickled ginger (optional), for serving

Instructions:

1. Prepare the Pork Cutlets (Tonkatsu):

- Season the pork cutlets with salt and pepper.
- Dredge each cutlet in flour, dip into beaten eggs, and coat thoroughly with panko breadcrumbs, pressing gently to adhere.
- Heat vegetable oil in a large skillet over medium heat. Fry the pork cutlets until golden brown and cooked through, about 3-4 minutes per side. Transfer to a plate lined with paper towels to drain excess oil. Cut into strips.

2. Make the Katsudon Sauce:

- In the same skillet (wipe out excess oil if necessary), add sliced onions and sauté until softened and translucent.
- Add dashi stock, soy sauce, mirin, and sugar. Bring to a simmer and cook for a few minutes until the flavors meld together.

3. Assemble Katsudon:

- Arrange the cooked pork cutlet strips evenly over the simmering sauce in the skillet.

- Pour beaten eggs evenly over the pork and sauce. Cover and simmer gently until the eggs are cooked to your liking, about 2-3 minutes for slightly runny yolks.
- Remove from heat.

4. Serve Katsudon:

- Scoop steamed rice into serving bowls.
- Carefully place the pork cutlet strips and egg mixture over the rice.
- Garnish with chopped green onions.
- Serve immediately, optionally with pickled ginger on the side.

Tips:

- **Rice:** Use Japanese short-grain rice for an authentic Katsudon experience. Cook rice according to package instructions for best results.
- **Sauce Consistency:** Adjust the thickness of the sauce by simmering longer for a thicker consistency or adding a cornstarch slurry (1 teaspoon cornstarch mixed with 1 tablespoon water) if needed.
- **Variations:** Some recipes include adding vegetables like sliced mushrooms or snow peas to the sauce for extra flavor and texture.
- **Leftovers:** Katsudon is best enjoyed fresh, but leftovers can be stored in an airtight container in the refrigerator and reheated gently in the microwave.

Katsudon is a comforting and satisfying dish that combines the crispy texture of tonkatsu with the richness of the egg and savory sauce, perfect for a hearty meal any time of the year. Enjoy making and savoring this classic Japanese rice bowl dish at home!

Ramen (Various Types)

Basic Ramen Components:

1. Broth:

- **Tonkotsu Broth:** Rich and creamy pork bone broth.
- **Shoyu Broth:** Clear broth flavored with soy sauce.
- **Miso Broth:** Broth made with miso paste for a savory, slightly sweet flavor.
- **Shio Broth:** Light and clear broth seasoned with salt.

2. Noodles:

- Fresh ramen noodles or dried noodles (typically alkaline noodles).
- Cook according to package instructions, then rinse with cold water to stop cooking and drain.

3. Toppings (Customizable):

- **Chashu:** Sliced braised pork belly.
- **Ajitsuke Tamago:** Soft-boiled marinated egg.
- **Negi:** Thinly sliced green onions.
- **Menma:** Seasoned bamboo shoots.
- **Nori:** Dried seaweed sheets.
- **Corn:** Sweet corn kernels.
- **Bean sprouts:** Fresh or blanched bean sprouts.
- **Kikurage:** Wood ear mushrooms.
- **Butter:** A knob of butter for added richness (common in miso ramen).

4. Optional Seasonings:

- **Soy Sauce:** Adds depth of flavor.
- **Mirin:** Sweet rice wine for a touch of sweetness.
- **Sesame oil:** Adds nutty flavor.
- **Chili oil or paste:** For heat and spice.
- **Garlic:** Minced garlic or garlic oil for aroma.

Basic Steps to Make Ramen:

1. Prepare the Broth:

- Choose your preferred broth type (tonkotsu, shoyu, miso, or shio).
- Simmer broth ingredients (pork bones for tonkotsu, chicken and vegetables for others) for several hours to extract flavors. Season to taste.

2. Cook the Noodles:

- Cook fresh or dried ramen noodles according to package instructions.
- Rinse cooked noodles with cold water to stop cooking and drain well.

3. Prepare Toppings:

- Cook chashu pork belly slices, boil and marinate eggs for ajitsuke tamago, and prepare other toppings as desired.

4. Assemble Ramen:

- Reheat cooked noodles by dipping briefly in hot water.
- Arrange noodles in bowls and ladle hot broth over them.
- Add toppings such as chashu, ajitsuke tamago, menma, nori, and green onions.

5. Garnish and Serve:

- Finish with additional seasonings like soy sauce, sesame oil, or chili oil as desired.
- Serve hot and enjoy immediately!

Popular Ramen Variations:

Tonkotsu Ramen:

- Features rich and creamy pork bone broth, topped with chashu pork, ajitsuke tamago, menma, and green onions.

Shoyu Ramen:

- Clear broth flavored with soy sauce, topped with chashu pork, menma, nori, and green onions.

Miso Ramen:

- Broth made with miso paste, topped with chashu pork, ajitsuke tamago, corn, and butter.

Shio Ramen:

- Light and clear broth seasoned with salt, topped with chashu pork, menma, kikurage mushrooms, and green onions.

Tips for Making Ramen:

- **Broth Simmering:** Take your time with simmering the broth to develop depth of flavor.
- **Noodle Cooking:** Cook noodles just before serving to ensure they remain chewy.
- **Customization:** Ramen is highly customizable—adjust toppings and seasonings to suit your taste preferences.
- **Presentation:** Arrange toppings neatly for an appealing presentation before serving.

Making ramen at home allows for creativity and personalization, making it a comforting and satisfying dish for any occasion. Enjoy exploring different ramen variations and flavors to find your favorite!

Oyakodon (Chicken and Egg Rice Bowl)

Ingredients:

- **For the Chicken and Egg Mixture:**
    - 2 boneless, skinless chicken thighs or breasts, thinly sliced
    - 1 onion, thinly sliced
    - 4 eggs
    - 1 tablespoon soy sauce
    - 1 tablespoon mirin (sweet rice wine)
    - 1 tablespoon sugar
    - 1 cup dashi stock (or substitute with chicken broth)
- **For Serving:**
    - Steamed Japanese rice
    - Chopped green onions or mitsuba (Japanese parsley) for garnish
    - Optional: Shichimi togarashi (Japanese seven-spice blend) for extra flavor

Instructions:

1. Prepare the Sauce:

- In a small bowl, mix together soy sauce, mirin, sugar, and dashi stock (or chicken broth). Set aside.

2. Cook Chicken and Onion:

- Heat a medium-sized skillet or pan over medium heat.
- Add thinly sliced onions and cook until softened and translucent, about 3-4 minutes.
- Add thinly sliced chicken to the skillet and cook until the chicken is no longer pink.

3. Add Sauce:

- Pour the prepared sauce over the chicken and onions in the skillet. Bring to a simmer and cook for another 3-4 minutes until the chicken is fully cooked and the sauce slightly thickens.

4. Add Eggs:

- In a small bowl, lightly beat the eggs.
- Slowly pour the beaten eggs over the chicken and sauce mixture in the skillet. Allow the eggs to distribute evenly.
- Cover the skillet with a lid and cook on low heat for about 2-3 minutes, or until the eggs are softly set.

5. Serve Oyakodon:

- Scoop steamed rice into serving bowls.
- Carefully spoon the chicken, egg, and onion mixture over the rice.
- Garnish with chopped green onions or mitsuba.
- Optionally, sprinkle with shichimi togarashi for added spice.

6. Enjoy:

- Serve Oyakodon hot and enjoy the savory combination of chicken, eggs, and sweet-savory sauce over rice.

Tips:

- **Dashi Substitute:** If you don't have dashi stock, you can use chicken broth or water with a dash of soy sauce for flavor.
- **Egg Doneness:** Cook the eggs to your preference—some prefer them softly set with a slightly runny yolk, while others prefer them fully cooked through.
- **Variations:** You can add other ingredients like mushrooms, peas, or spinach to customize your Oyakodon.
- **Leftovers:** Oyakodon is best enjoyed fresh, but leftovers can be refrigerated and reheated gently in the microwave.

Oyakodon is a comforting one-bowl meal that's popular in Japanese households for its simplicity and delicious flavors. Enjoy making and savoring this classic Chicken and Egg Rice Bowl dish at home!

Nikujaga (Meat and Potato Stew)

Ingredients:

- **For the Stew:**
    - 1/2 lb thinly sliced beef (such as ribeye or sirloin)
    - 2 medium potatoes, peeled and cut into chunks
    - 1 onion, thinly sliced
    - 1 carrot, peeled and sliced into rounds
    - 1/2 cup shirataki noodles (optional, rinsed and drained)
    - 2 cups dashi stock (or substitute with beef or vegetable broth)
    - 2 tablespoons soy sauce
    - 2 tablespoons mirin (sweet rice wine)
    - 1 tablespoon sugar
    - 1 tablespoon vegetable oil
- **For Garnish:**
    - Chopped green onions or mitsuba (Japanese parsley), for garnish

Instructions:

1. Prepare the Ingredients:

- Heat vegetable oil in a large pot or deep skillet over medium heat.
- Add thinly sliced beef and cook until browned.

2. Add Vegetables:

- Add sliced onions and carrots to the pot. Stir and cook until onions are softened.

3. Simmer with Sauce:

- Add dashi stock (or broth), soy sauce, mirin, and sugar to the pot. Stir well to combine.
- Bring to a boil, then reduce heat to low and simmer uncovered for about 10 minutes.

4. Add Potatoes and Shirataki:

- Add potato chunks and shirataki noodles (if using) to the pot.
- Stir to combine, making sure the potatoes are submerged in the liquid.

5. Simmer Until Potatoes are Tender:

- Cover the pot and simmer on low heat for about 20-25 minutes, or until the potatoes are tender and cooked through.

6. Adjust Seasoning:

- Taste and adjust seasoning with more soy sauce or sugar if desired.

7. Serve Nikujaga:

- Spoon Nikujaga into serving bowls.
- Garnish with chopped green onions or mitsuba.

8. Enjoy:

- Serve Nikujaga hot over steamed rice as a main dish. It's comforting and perfect for a family meal.

Tips:

- **Dashi Substitute:** If you don't have dashi stock, you can use beef or vegetable broth. Dashi adds a traditional Japanese flavor, but other broths work well too.
- **Meat Selection:** Thinly sliced beef is traditional, but you can also use pork or chicken if preferred.
- **Vegetable Variations:** Some variations include adding green beans, snap peas, or mushrooms for additional texture and flavor.
- **Leftovers:** Nikujaga tastes even better the next day as the flavors meld together. Store leftovers in an airtight container in the refrigerator and reheat gently.

Nikujaga is a hearty and satisfying dish that combines tender meat, potatoes, and vegetables in a deliciously savory sauce. It's a wonderful introduction to Japanese home cooking and perfect for enjoying with steamed rice.

Hiyashi Chuka (Cold Ramen Salad)

Ingredients:

- **For the Sesame Dressing:**
    - 3 tablespoons soy sauce
    - 2 tablespoons rice vinegar
    - 1 tablespoon sesame oil
    - 1 tablespoon sugar
    - 1 teaspoon grated ginger
    - 1 teaspoon sesame seeds
- **For the Ramen Noodles:**
    - 4 servings of fresh or dried ramen noodles (about 400g)
    - Water for boiling
    - Ice water (for cooling and rinsing noodles)
- **For Toppings (Customizable):**
    - Thinly sliced cucumber
    - Thinly sliced carrots
    - Thinly sliced bell peppers (red, yellow, or orange)
    - Shredded lettuce or spinach
    - Cooked and shredded chicken, ham, or imitation crab sticks
    - Thin omelette strips (optional)
    - Cherry tomatoes, halved
    - Toasted sesame seeds, for garnish
    - Nori (seaweed), cut into thin strips

Instructions:

1. Prepare the Sesame Dressing:

- In a small bowl, whisk together soy sauce, rice vinegar, sesame oil, sugar, grated ginger, and sesame seeds until well combined. Set aside.

2. Cook the Ramen Noodles:

- Bring a large pot of water to a boil. Cook the ramen noodles according to package instructions (usually 3-4 minutes for fresh noodles, or as per the package for dried noodles).
- Drain the noodles and immediately rinse under cold running water or plunge into ice water to stop the cooking process and cool them down. Drain well.

3. Assemble Hiyashi Chuka:

- Divide the cooled noodles among serving bowls.

- Arrange the assorted toppings (cucumber, carrots, bell peppers, lettuce or spinach, shredded chicken or ham, omelette strips, cherry tomatoes) on top of the noodles in an attractive pattern.

4. Serve with Sesame Dressing:

- Drizzle the sesame dressing generously over the noodles and toppings.
- Garnish with toasted sesame seeds and nori strips.

5. Enjoy:

- Serve Hiyashi Chuka immediately and enjoy the refreshing flavors and textures!

Tips:

- **Customize Toppings:** Feel free to customize Hiyashi Chuka with your favorite vegetables, proteins, or seafood.
- **Make-Ahead:** Prepare the noodles, toppings, and dressing ahead of time and assemble just before serving for a quick meal.
- **Chilling:** For best results, chill the assembled Hiyashi Chuka in the refrigerator for about 30 minutes before serving to enhance the flavors and texture.
- **Leftovers:** Store any leftover noodles and toppings separately from the dressing to prevent them from becoming soggy. Assemble fresh before serving again.

Hiyashi Chuka is a delightful dish that offers a cool and refreshing twist on traditional ramen, making it a perfect choice for summer lunches or light dinners. Enjoy this Japanese cold noodle salad as a delicious and healthy meal option!

Ankimo (Monkfish Liver)

Ingredients:

- **For Steaming:**
    - 1 monkfish liver (ankimo)
    - Salt for seasoning
- **For Serving:**
    - Ponzu sauce (or soy sauce mixed with citrus juice)
    - Grated daikon radish
    - Chopped green onions

Instructions:

1. Prepare the Monkfish Liver (Ankimo):

- If you have purchased fresh monkfish liver, it may come already cleaned and prepped. If not, you'll need to clean it by removing any membranes or blood vessels.

2. Season and Steam:

- Sprinkle the monkfish liver generously with salt on all sides.
- Wrap the liver tightly in plastic wrap or cheesecloth to form a cylindrical shape, ensuring it is tightly secured.
- Steam the wrapped monkfish liver for about 20-30 minutes until it becomes firm and cooked through. You can test doneness by inserting a skewer or toothpick; it should come out clean when done.

3. Chill:

- Remove the steamed ankimo from the steamer and let it cool to room temperature. Then, refrigerate it for at least 2 hours or until completely chilled. This helps the flavors to develop and the liver to firm up.

4. Serve Ankimo:

- Unwrap the chilled ankimo and slice it into thin rounds or diagonal slices.
- Arrange the ankimo slices on a serving plate.
- Serve with ponzu sauce for dipping (or a mixture of soy sauce and citrus juice), grated daikon radish, and chopped green onions.

5. Enjoy:

- Ankimo is traditionally enjoyed as a cold appetizer. It has a delicate, creamy texture and a subtle umami flavor that pairs well with the tangy ponzu sauce and refreshing grated daikon radish.

Tips:

- **Freshness:** Purchase fresh monkfish liver from a reputable fishmonger for the best quality and flavor.
- **Steaming:** Be careful not to overcook the ankimo; it should be firm yet tender after steaming.
- **Presentation:** Arrange the sliced ankimo neatly on the serving plate for an appealing presentation.
- **Variations:** Some prefer to lightly sear the slices of ankimo in a hot pan for a caramelized exterior before serving.

Ankimo is a unique and luxurious delicacy in Japanese cuisine, often savored for its velvety texture and subtle taste. Enjoy making and serving this traditional appetizer to impress your guests or to indulge in a special culinary experience at home.

Agedashi Tofu (Deep Fried Tofu)

Ingredients:

- **For the Tofu:**
    - 1 block (14-16 oz) firm tofu
    - Cornstarch or potato starch for dusting
    - Vegetable oil for deep-frying
- **For the Dashi-Based Sauce:**
    - 1 cup dashi stock (or substitute with vegetable broth)
    - 2 tablespoons soy sauce
    - 1 tablespoon mirin (sweet rice wine)
    - 1 teaspoon sugar
- **For Garnish:**
    - Grated daikon radish
    - Bonito flakes (katsuobushi)
    - Chopped green onions
    - Shichimi togarashi (Japanese seven-spice blend) (optional)

Instructions:

1. Prepare the Tofu:

- Drain the tofu from its package and pat dry with paper towels.
- Cut the tofu into cubes or rectangles, about 1-inch thick.

2. Coat and Fry the Tofu:

- Heat vegetable oil in a deep skillet or pot to 350°F (180°C).
- Lightly dust each tofu piece with cornstarch or potato starch, shaking off any excess.
- Carefully lower the tofu pieces into the hot oil, in batches if necessary, and fry until golden brown and crispy, about 2-3 minutes per side. Remove and drain on paper towels.

3. Make the Dashi-Based Sauce:

- In a small saucepan, combine dashi stock, soy sauce, mirin, and sugar.
- Bring to a simmer over medium heat, stirring occasionally, until the sugar dissolves and the sauce slightly thickens. Remove from heat.

4. Serve Agedashi Tofu:

- Arrange the fried tofu pieces on serving plates.
- Spoon the hot dashi-based sauce over the tofu pieces.

5. Garnish and Enjoy:

- Garnish each tofu piece with grated daikon radish, bonito flakes, and chopped green onions.
- Optionally, sprinkle with shichimi togarashi for added spice.
- Serve Agedashi Tofu immediately while hot and crispy.

Tips:

- **Tofu Preparation:** Use firm tofu for Agedashi Tofu to ensure it holds its shape during frying.
- **Frying Temperature:** Maintain a consistent oil temperature around 350°F (180°C) to achieve crispy tofu without it absorbing too much oil.
- **Dashi Stock:** Traditional dashi stock adds authentic Japanese flavor, but you can substitute with vegetable broth for a vegetarian version.
- **Presentation:** Arrange the tofu pieces neatly on the plate and drizzle the sauce generously over them for a beautiful presentation.

Agedashi Tofu is a delightful appetizer that showcases the versatility of tofu in Japanese cuisine. Enjoy its crispy exterior, tender interior, and savory dashi-based sauce with traditional garnishes for a satisfying and flavorful dish.

Matsutake Gohan (Matsutake Rice)

Ingredients:

- **For Cooking Rice:**
    - 2 cups Japanese short-grain rice
    - 2 cups dashi stock (or substitute with vegetable or chicken broth)
    - 1-2 matsutake mushrooms, cleaned and thinly sliced
    - 1 tablespoon soy sauce
    - 1 tablespoon sake
    - 1 tablespoon mirin (sweet rice wine)
    - Salt, to taste
- **Optional Garnish:**
    - Chopped green onions or mitsuba (Japanese parsley)

Instructions:

1. Prepare the Matsutake Mushrooms:

- Clean the matsutake mushrooms with a damp cloth to remove any dirt. Trim off the tough base and thinly slice the mushrooms.

2. Rinse and Soak the Rice:

- Rinse the rice under cold water until the water runs clear.
- Soak the rinsed rice in water for about 30 minutes, then drain well.

3. Cook the Rice:

- In a medium-sized pot or rice cooker, combine the drained rice and dashi stock.
- Add soy sauce, sake, mirin, and a pinch of salt. Stir gently to combine.
- Arrange the sliced matsutake mushrooms on top of the rice mixture.

4. Cook the Rice:

- Cook the rice according to your rice cooker's instructions or on the stovetop. If using a rice cooker, set it to the regular rice cooking mode. If cooking on the stovetop, bring the mixture to a boil over medium-high heat, then reduce the heat to low, cover, and simmer for about 15-20 minutes, or until the rice is tender and the liquid is absorbed.

5. Let the Rice Rest:

- Once the rice is cooked, let it rest for 10 minutes off the heat with the lid on. This helps to steam the rice and matsutake mushrooms evenly.

6. Serve Matsutake Gohan:

- Fluff the rice gently with a rice paddle or fork.
- Transfer Matsutake Gohan to a serving bowl or individual bowls.
- Garnish with chopped green onions or mitsuba for added freshness and color.

7. Enjoy:

- Serve Matsutake Gohan hot as a delicious side dish or main course, highlighting the aromatic flavor of matsutake mushrooms and the umami of dashi stock.

Tips:

- **Matsutake Mushrooms:** Use fresh matsutake mushrooms when they are in season for the best flavor. If fresh matsutake mushrooms are not available, you can also use dried matsutake mushrooms that have been rehydrated.
- **Rice Consistency:** Adjust the amount of dashi stock slightly based on your preference for softer or firmer rice.
- **Variation:** Some recipes may include additional ingredients such as ginkgo nuts or chestnuts for added texture and flavor.

Matsutake Gohan is a special dish in Japanese cuisine that celebrates the seasonal availability of matsutake mushrooms. Enjoy its delicate aroma and delicious flavor as part of a Japanese meal or on its own as a delightful culinary experience.

Chashu (Roasted Pork)

Ingredients:

- **For the Chashu:**
    - 1 lb pork belly or pork shoulder, skin removed
    - 1/2 cup soy sauce
    - 1/2 cup mirin (sweet rice wine)
    - 1/2 cup sake (Japanese rice wine) or dry sherry
    - 1/4 cup sugar
    - 3-4 slices ginger
    - 2 cloves garlic, smashed
    - 2 green onions, chopped
    - 2 cups water (or enough to cover the pork)

Instructions:

1. Prepare the Pork:

- If using pork belly, cut it into a rectangular shape for easier rolling. If using pork shoulder, cut it into a rectangular shape as well.

2. Roll and Tie the Pork:

- Roll up the pork tightly from one end and secure it with kitchen twine at regular intervals to maintain its shape during cooking.

3. Braise the Pork:

- In a large pot or Dutch oven, combine soy sauce, mirin, sake, sugar, ginger slices, smashed garlic cloves, and chopped green onions.
- Add enough water to cover the pork completely.
- Bring the mixture to a boil over medium-high heat, then reduce the heat to low and simmer, covered, for about 2-3 hours or until the pork is tender and cooked through. Turn the pork occasionally during cooking.

4. Cool and Marinate:

- Once cooked, remove the pot from heat and let the pork cool in the braising liquid to absorb more flavors.

5. Slice and Serve:

- Remove the pork from the braising liquid and discard the twine.
- Slice the pork thinly against the grain.

6. Optional Step - Char and Glaze (for Char Siu style):

- Preheat the broiler (or grill if using an outdoor grill).
- Place the sliced pork on a baking sheet lined with foil.
- Brush the pork slices with a mixture of honey and soy sauce.
- Broil or grill the pork slices until the edges are slightly charred and caramelized, basting occasionally with the honey-soy mixture.

7. Serve Chashu:

- Serve Chashu slices as a topping for ramen, rice bowls, or as a side dish.
- Optionally, drizzle with some of the braising liquid or serve with additional soy sauce and chopped green onions.

Tips:

- **Preparation Time:** You can prepare Chashu ahead of time and store it in the refrigerator in its braising liquid. This allows the flavors to deepen even further.
- **Braising Liquid:** The braising liquid can be strained and used as a flavorful base for soups or sauces.
- **Variations:** Some recipes may include additional ingredients such as star anise, cinnamon, or Chinese five-spice powder for extra flavor complexity.

Chashu is a delicious and versatile dish that adds richness and flavor to various Japanese dishes, especially ramen. Enjoy making this traditional Japanese roasted pork at home and savor its tender texture and savory-sweet taste!

Natto (Fermented Soybeans)

Ingredients:

- **For Serving:**
    - Natto (fermented soybeans)
    - Soy sauce (to taste)
    - Mustard (typically included with natto)
    - Cooked rice
    - Optional toppings: chopped green onions, shredded nori (seaweed), grated daikon radish

Instructions:

1. Prepare Natto:

- Open the package of natto and remove the plastic wrap covering the beans.
- Inside, you'll find a packet of soy sauce and mustard. Add these to the natto according to your taste preference. The mustard helps to cut through the strong flavor and aroma of the beans.

2. Mix Natto:

- Using chopsticks or a fork, vigorously stir the natto to mix it well. This step also helps to create the characteristic sticky and slimy texture of natto.

3. Serve Natto:

- Serve the mixed natto over a bowl of hot steamed rice. It's a common breakfast dish in Japan, but it can be enjoyed at any mealtime.
- Optionally, garnish with chopped green onions, shredded nori, or grated daikon radish for additional flavor and texture.

4. Enjoy:

- Mix the natto and rice together thoroughly before eating. The combination of flavors and textures is unique and may take some getting used to if you're trying it for the first time.

Tips:

- **Accompaniments:** Natto is often served with additional condiments like soy sauce, mustard, and toppings to enhance its flavor and texture.
- **Texture:** The slimy texture of natto is characteristic of its fermentation process and is considered desirable in Japanese cuisine.

- **Nutritional Benefits:** Natto is rich in protein, probiotics, and vitamin K2, making it a nutritious addition to a balanced diet.
- **Pairing:** Natto pairs well with other traditional Japanese breakfast items like miso soup and pickled vegetables.

Natto is an acquired taste, but it's worth trying if you're interested in exploring authentic Japanese cuisine and its diverse flavors. Enjoy it as a nutritious and unique dish that offers a glimpse into Japan's rich culinary heritage.

Fugu (Blowfish)

Ingredients:

- Fresh fugu (blowfish) fillets, properly cleaned and prepared by a licensed chef
- Soy sauce
- Wasabi (Japanese horseradish)
- Sliced green onions (optional, for garnish)
- Shiso leaves (optional, for garnish)

Instructions:

1. **Preparation:**
   - Ensure the fugu fillets have been thoroughly cleaned by a licensed chef, removing all toxic parts such as the liver, ovaries, and skin.
   - The fillets should be sliced very thinly with a sharp knife, similar to sashimi style.
2. **Presentation:**
   - Arrange the sliced fugu on a chilled plate or platter.
   - Optionally, garnish with sliced green onions and shiso leaves for added flavor and presentation.
3. **Serving:**
   - Serve immediately with small dishes of soy sauce and wasabi on the side.
   - Dip the fugu slices lightly into soy sauce mixed with a small amount of wasabi before eating.

Important Notes:

- **Safety Warning:** Only consume fugu that has been prepared by a licensed chef. The toxins in improperly prepared fugu can be lethal.
- **Legal Considerations:** In many countries, including Japan, it is illegal to prepare or serve fugu without the appropriate license due to safety concerns.
- **Expertise Required:** This recipe assumes the fugu has been prepared by a highly trained professional. Please do not attempt to prepare fugu at home without proper certification and knowledge.

While fugu is a revered delicacy in Japan, it is crucial to respect the strict regulations and safety measures in place for its preparation and consumption.

Kakiage (Mixed Vegetable Tempura)

Ingredients:

- Assorted vegetables (such as onions, carrots, sweet potatoes, bell peppers, zucchini, mushrooms, green beans, etc.)
- Tempura batter mix (available in Japanese grocery stores) or you can make your own with flour, cornstarch, baking powder, and cold water
- Oil for deep-frying (vegetable oil or canola oil)
- Salt for seasoning
- Tempura dipping sauce (tsuyu) or tentsuyu (a mixture of soy sauce, mirin, and dashi stock) for serving

Instructions:

1. **Prepare the Vegetables:**
   - Peel and thinly slice the vegetables into julienne strips. Try to keep the slices uniform in size for even cooking.
   - You can mix and match vegetables according to your preference. Common choices include onions, carrots, sweet potatoes, bell peppers, zucchini, mushrooms, and green beans.
2. **Make the Tempura Batter:**
   - Follow the instructions on the tempura batter mix package, or if making from scratch, combine flour, cornstarch, baking powder, and cold water in a bowl. Mix until you get a smooth, thin batter. It should be the consistency of thin pancake batter.
3. **Heat the Oil:**
   - Heat oil in a deep frying pan or a deep fryer to around 350°F (175°C). The oil should be hot enough that a drop of batter sizzles and floats to the surface immediately without browning too quickly.
4. **Coat and Fry the Vegetables:**
   - Dip a handful of the prepared vegetables into the tempura batter, coating them evenly.
   - Carefully lower the battered vegetables into the hot oil, making sure not to overcrowd the pan. Fry in batches if necessary.
   - Fry the kakiage for 2-3 minutes or until they are golden brown and crispy. Use chopsticks or a slotted spoon to gently turn them for even cooking.
5. **Drain and Season:**
   - Once the kakiage are golden and crispy, remove them from the oil and drain on a paper towel-lined plate to absorb excess oil.
   - Immediately sprinkle with a pinch of salt while they are still hot to enhance the flavor.
6. **Serve:**

- Serve the kakiage hot with tempura dipping sauce (tsuyu) or tentsuyu on the side for dipping. You can also enjoy them with a sprinkle of grated daikon radish or a squeeze of lemon juice.

Tips:

- To ensure crispy tempura, keep the batter cold and refrain from over-mixing.
- Fry vegetables in small batches to maintain oil temperature and prevent them from sticking together.
- Adjust the thickness of the batter according to your preference for a lighter or thicker coating.

Kakiage is best enjoyed immediately after frying when they are at their crispiest. It's a delightful dish that showcases the natural flavors and textures of a variety of vegetables in a light and crispy tempura batter.

Hiroshima Okonomiyaki

Ingredients:

- Okonomiyaki batter mix (available at Japanese grocery stores) or you can make your own with flour, dashi stock or water, baking powder, and eggs
- Cabbage, thinly sliced (about 2 cups)
- Bean sprouts (optional)
- Thinly sliced pork belly or bacon (about 4-6 slices per okonomiyaki)
- Yakisoba noodles (about 1 bundle per okonomiyaki)
- Eggs (1-2 per okonomiyaki)
- Okonomiyaki sauce (available in Japanese grocery stores or homemade with Worcestershire sauce, ketchup, soy sauce, and sugar)
- Japanese mayonnaise (Kewpie brand is traditional, but any mayonnaise will work)
- Aonori (dried seaweed flakes)
- Katsuobushi (bonito flakes)
- Pickled ginger (optional, for serving)

Instructions:

1. **Prepare the Yakisoba Noodles:**
   - Cook the yakisoba noodles according to package instructions (usually boiled for a few minutes until tender), then drain and set aside. You can also use precooked yakisoba noodles for convenience.
2. **Prepare the Okonomiyaki Batter:**
   - Follow the instructions on the okonomiyaki batter mix package, or if making from scratch, combine flour, dashi stock or water, baking powder, and eggs in a bowl. Mix until smooth and slightly thick, similar to pancake batter.
3. **Cooking the Layers:**
   - Heat a large non-stick frying pan or griddle over medium heat. Add a little oil and spread thinly sliced cabbage (and bean sprouts, if using) evenly over the pan to form a round shape slightly larger than your desired okonomiyaki size.
   - Pour a ladleful of the okonomiyaki batter over the cabbage, spreading it to cover the vegetables evenly. Let it cook for a few minutes until the bottom starts to set.
4. **Add the Pork Belly or Bacon:**
   - Place slices of pork belly or bacon on top of the okonomiyaki batter. Let it cook until the bottom is golden brown and the pork is cooked through.
5. **Cook the Eggs:**
   - Push the cooked cabbage and pork to one side of the pan. Crack 1-2 eggs (depending on your preference) onto the empty side of the pan and scramble them until just cooked.
6. **Assemble the Okonomiyaki:**
   - Once the eggs are cooked, carefully slide the cooked yakisoba noodles on top of the cabbage and pork layer. Use a spatula to fold the cabbage layer over the noodles and egg, creating a neat stack.

7. **Final Assembly:**
    - Drizzle okonomiyaki sauce generously over the top of the okonomiyaki.
    - Squeeze zigzag lines of Japanese mayonnaise over the sauce.
    - Sprinkle aonori (dried seaweed flakes) and katsuobushi (bonito flakes) on top for added flavor and texture.
8. **Serve:**
    - Transfer the Hiroshima-style Okonomiyaki to a plate and serve immediately while hot.
    - Optionally, garnish with pickled ginger on the side for a refreshing bite between each savory bite.

Enjoy this layered and flavorful Hiroshima-style Okonomiyaki as a satisfying meal that combines the richness of pork, the crunch of cabbage, the savory-sweetness of okonomiyaki sauce, and the creamy tang of Japanese mayonnaise. It's a beloved dish that offers a unique culinary experience!

Tai Sashimi (Sea Bream Sashimi)

Ingredients:

- Fresh sea bream (tai) fillets, preferably sushi-grade
- Soy sauce, for dipping
- Wasabi (Japanese horseradish), for serving
- Freshly grated ginger, for serving (optional)
- Shiso leaves or thinly sliced green onions, for garnish (optional)

Instructions:

1. **Selecting and Preparing the Sea Bream:**
   - Ensure the sea bream fillets are fresh and sushi-grade, meaning they are safe to consume raw. It's best to purchase from a reputable fishmonger or Japanese grocery store.
2. **Slicing the Sea Bream:**
   - Use a very sharp knife to slice the sea bream fillets into thin slices. Angle the knife slightly to achieve slices that are about 1/8 to 1/4 inch thick. The slices should be delicate and almost translucent.
3. **Arranging the Sashimi:**
   - Arrange the sea bream slices neatly on a chilled plate or platter. You can arrange them in a single layer or slightly overlapping, depending on your preference.
4. **Garnishing and Serving:**
   - Serve the tai sashimi immediately after slicing.
   - Accompany the sashimi with small dishes of soy sauce and wasabi.
   - Optionally, serve freshly grated ginger for a bit of spicy warmth.
   - Garnish with shiso leaves or thinly sliced green onions for added flavor and visual appeal.
5. **Enjoying Tai Sashimi:**
   - To eat, dip a slice of sea bream into the soy sauce mixed with a small amount of wasabi.
   - Enjoy the tai sashimi with a balance of the fish's natural sweetness and the salty umami of the soy sauce.

Tips:

- **Freshness is Key:** Since tai sashimi is enjoyed raw, freshness is crucial. Ensure the fish is properly handled and stored at appropriate temperatures.
- **Sharp Knife:** Use a sharp, long knife for slicing the sea bream. A dull knife can damage the delicate texture of the fish.
- **Presentation:** Tai sashimi is often served on traditional Japanese ceramic or lacquerware plates, which enhance the aesthetic appeal of the dish.

Tai sashimi is a delightful dish that allows you to savor the pure, fresh taste of sea bream. Enjoy it as a starter or part of a larger Japanese meal, paired with other sashimi varieties or sushi for a complete culinary experience.

Kani Miso (Crab Miso Soup)

Ingredients:

- 2 cups dashi stock (you can use dashi powder or make dashi from kombu and katsuobushi)
- 100 grams fresh crab meat (cooked and picked)
- 2 tablespoons miso paste (white or red miso, adjust to taste)
- 1 green onion, finely chopped
- 1 block silken tofu, cut into small cubes (optional)
- 1 tablespoon soy sauce (optional, for seasoning)

Instructions:

1. **Prepare Dashi Stock:**
    - If you're using dashi powder, follow the instructions on the package to make 2 cups of dashi stock. If making from scratch, soak a piece of kombu (dried kelp) in 2 cups of water for about 30 minutes, then gently heat the water until just before boiling. Remove the kombu and add 1/4 cup of katsuobushi (bonito flakes). Let it steep for 5 minutes, then strain the liquid to make dashi stock.
2. **Prepare Crab Meat:**
    - Cook fresh crab meat if it's not already cooked. Remove the meat from the shells and set aside.
3. **Make Kani Miso Soup:**
    - In a medium saucepan, bring the dashi stock to a gentle simmer over medium heat.
    - Add the crab meat to the simmering dashi stock and let it heat through for about 1-2 minutes.
4. **Dissolve Miso Paste:**
    - In a small bowl, dissolve the miso paste in a small amount of dashi stock or hot water to make it easier to mix into the soup. Stir until smooth.
5. **Add Miso Paste to Soup:**
    - Lower the heat to low. Add the dissolved miso paste to the soup, stirring gently to incorporate. Avoid boiling the soup once miso has been added to preserve its flavor.
6. **Add Tofu and Seasoning (Optional):**
    - If using tofu, gently add the cubed tofu to the soup and let it warm through for another minute.
    - Taste the soup and adjust the flavor with soy sauce if desired, though be cautious as miso is already salty.
7. **Serve:**
    - Ladle the Kani Miso Soup into bowls. Garnish with finely chopped green onions.
8. **Enjoy:**
    - Serve Kani Miso Soup hot as a comforting appetizer or part of a Japanese meal. It pairs well with steamed rice and other dishes.

Tips:

- **Quality of Miso:** The flavor of Kani Miso Soup heavily depends on the quality and type of miso used. White miso tends to be milder and sweeter, while red miso is more robust and salty. Adjust the amount of miso paste according to your preference.
- **Variations:** You can customize Kani Miso Soup by adding other ingredients like mushrooms, spinach, or seaweed (such as wakame) for added flavor and texture.

Kani Miso Soup is a delightful way to enjoy the natural sweetness of crab in a warm, comforting broth. It's a popular dish in Japanese cuisine, especially during colder months, offering a taste of umami-rich flavors from the sea.

Ika Geso Karaage (Deep Fried Squid Tentacles)

Ingredients:

- Squid tentacles (ika geso), cleaned and separated
- Cornstarch or potato starch, for coating
- Vegetable oil, for deep-frying
- Salt and pepper, to taste
- Lemon wedges, for serving
- Optional: Shichimi togarashi (Japanese seven-spice blend), for added spice

Instructions:

1. **Prepare the Squid Tentacles:**
   - Ensure the squid tentacles are cleaned thoroughly. Rinse them under cold water and pat dry with paper towels.
2. **Coat with Cornstarch:**
   - Place the cleaned squid tentacles in a bowl. Season lightly with salt and pepper.
   - Coat the squid tentacles evenly with cornstarch or potato starch. Shake off any excess starch.
3. **Heat the Oil:**
   - In a deep frying pan or pot, heat vegetable oil to around 350°F (175°C). Use enough oil to submerge the squid tentacles for deep-frying.
4. **Fry the Squid Tentacles:**
   - Carefully add the coated squid tentacles to the hot oil, a few at a time to avoid overcrowding the pan. Fry in batches if necessary.
   - Fry the squid tentacles for about 2-3 minutes, or until they are golden brown and crispy. Stir gently with chopsticks or a slotted spoon to ensure even cooking.
5. **Drain and Serve:**
   - Once the squid tentacles are crispy and golden, remove them from the oil and drain on a paper towel-lined plate to remove excess oil.
6. **Season and Serve:**
   - Season the fried squid tentacles with a pinch of salt and pepper while they are still hot.
   - Serve Ika Geso Karaage immediately with lemon wedges on the side for squeezing over the crispy tentacles.
   - Optionally, sprinkle with shichimi togarashi for added spice and flavor.
7. **Enjoy:**
   - Enjoy Ika Geso Karaage as a delicious appetizer or side dish. It pairs well with a cold beer or Japanese sake.

Tips:

- **Freshness of Squid:** Ensure the squid tentacles are fresh for the best flavor and texture.

- **Oil Temperature:** Maintain the oil temperature around 350°F (175°C) for crispy results without burning the coating.
- **Handling Hot Oil:** Use caution when frying to avoid splattering hot oil. Fry in small batches and use a slotted spoon or mesh strainer to remove the squid tentacles from the oil.

Ika Geso Karaage is a crispy and addictive dish that showcases the unique texture and flavor of squid tentacles. It's a popular izakaya (Japanese pub) dish that can be enjoyed as part of a Japanese meal or as a snack with drinks.

Zaru Soba (Cold Buckwheat Noodles)

Ingredients:

- Soba noodles (buckwheat noodles)
- Zaru Soba dipping sauce (Tsuyu) - available in Japanese grocery stores or homemade (recipe below)
- Toppings: Thinly sliced green onions, shredded nori (seaweed), grated daikon radish, wasabi (optional), sesame seeds (optional)

For the Zaru Soba Dipping Sauce (Tsuyu):

- 1 cup dashi stock (you can use dashi powder or make dashi from kombu and katsuobushi)
- 1/4 cup soy sauce
- 1/4 cup mirin (sweet rice wine)
- 1 tablespoon sugar

Instructions:

1. **Prepare the Zaru Soba Dipping Sauce (Tsuyu):**
   - If making from scratch, combine dashi stock, soy sauce, mirin, and sugar in a saucepan. Bring to a boil, then simmer for a few minutes to blend the flavors. Let it cool, then chill in the refrigerator until ready to use.
2. **Cook the Soba Noodles:**
   - Bring a large pot of water to a boil. Cook the soba noodles according to the package instructions (usually 4-5 minutes) or until al dente.
   - Stir the noodles occasionally to prevent sticking. Avoid overcooking as soba noodles can become mushy quickly.
3. **Rinse and Drain the Noodles:**
   - Once cooked, drain the soba noodles and rinse well under cold running water until they are completely cool. This stops the cooking process and removes excess starch.
4. **Prepare the Toppings:**
   - Prepare your desired toppings such as thinly sliced green onions, shredded nori (seaweed), grated daikon radish, wasabi, and sesame seeds. Arrange them in small serving bowls.
5. **Serve Zaru Soba:**
   - Divide the cold soba noodles among serving plates or bamboo baskets (traditional zaru soba baskets if available).
   - Serve the chilled Zaru Soba dipping sauce (Tsuyu) in individual small bowls.
   - Optionally, add a small amount of wasabi to the dipping sauce for extra spice.
6. **Enjoy Zaru Soba:**
   - To eat, take a portion of soba noodles with chopsticks and dip them into the Zaru Soba dipping sauce (Tsuyu).

- Enjoy the cold soba noodles with the refreshing dipping sauce and your choice of toppings. Mix and match toppings as you like for different flavors and textures.

Tips:

- **Quality of Soba Noodles:** Use high-quality soba noodles for the best texture and flavor. Look for noodles made with a higher percentage of buckwheat (ideally 100% buckwheat noodles for a more traditional taste).
- **Chilling Noodles:** Chilling the cooked soba noodles in ice water after rinsing can help them stay firm and chewy.
- **Variations:** Zaru Soba can be customized with additional toppings such as tempura flakes (tenkasu), sliced cucumber, or grated ginger.

Zaru Soba is a delightful and healthy dish that's simple to prepare at home. It's a popular choice in Japan for its clean flavors and cooling effect, making it perfect for hot weather or as a light meal.

Yudofu (Tofu Hot Pot)

Ingredients:

- 1 block (about 14 oz or 400g) of firm tofu
- 4 cups water
- 1 piece kombu (dried kelp), about 4 inches square
- Soy sauce, for serving
- Ponzu sauce (optional), for serving
- Thinly sliced green onions (optional), for garnish
- Grated ginger (optional), for garnish

Instructions:

1. **Prepare the Kombu Broth:**
    - In a large pot, add 4 cups of water and the piece of kombu (dried kelp). Let it soak for about 30 minutes to extract flavor from the kombu.
2. **Simmer the Kombu Broth:**
    - Place the pot over medium heat and slowly bring the kombu broth to a gentle simmer. Avoid boiling the broth to preserve its delicate flavor.
3. **Prepare the Tofu:**
    - While the broth is heating, cut the tofu block into bite-sized cubes or slices.
4. **Add Tofu to the Broth:**
    - Once the kombu broth is simmering, carefully add the tofu cubes/slices to the pot. Allow them to simmer gently in the broth for about 5-7 minutes, or until heated through.
5. **Serve Yudofu:**
    - Ladle the hot yudofu and broth into individual serving bowls, making sure to distribute the tofu evenly.
    - Serve Yudofu hot, accompanied by small dishes of soy sauce and ponzu sauce (if using) for dipping.
    - Optionally, garnish with thinly sliced green onions and grated ginger on top of each serving.
6. **Enjoy Yudofu:**
    - To eat, dip the tofu pieces into the soy sauce or ponzu sauce before enjoying. The broth can be sipped on its own or used as a light soup.

Tips:

- **Variations:** Yudofu can be customized with additional ingredients such as shiitake mushrooms, spinach, or enoki mushrooms for added flavor and texture.
- **Serving Suggestions:** Yudofu is often served as part of a larger meal with rice and other side dishes, or as a standalone dish for a light and nourishing meal.
- **Quality of Ingredients:** Use good quality tofu and kombu for the best flavor. Soft or silken tofu can also be used for a different texture.

Yudofu is a comforting and healthy dish that highlights the simplicity and purity of tofu and kombu. It's a wonderful option for vegetarians and those looking for a light yet satisfying meal in Japanese cuisine.

Shojin Ryori (Buddhist Vegetarian Cuisine)

Ingredients:

- 1 cup white sesame seeds
- 2 tablespoons kudzu starch (or arrowroot starch)
- 1 1/2 cups water
- 1/2 teaspoon salt
- Soy sauce, for serving
- Wasabi (Japanese horseradish), for serving
- Thinly sliced green onions, for garnish (optional)

Instructions:

1. **Prepare the Sesame Seeds:**
   - Toast the white sesame seeds in a dry skillet over medium heat until fragrant and lightly golden. Be careful not to burn them. Remove from heat and let them cool.
2. **Grind the Sesame Seeds:**
   - Grind the toasted sesame seeds in a suribachi (Japanese mortar and pestle) or a food processor until they form a smooth paste. This may take several minutes of grinding or processing.
3. **Make Sesame Paste:**
   - In a small saucepan, combine the ground sesame seeds with water and stir well to combine.
4. **Cook the Sesame Paste:**
   - Heat the sesame paste mixture over medium heat, stirring constantly. Gradually sprinkle in the kudzu starch (or arrowroot starch) while stirring to prevent lumps from forming.
5. **Simmer and Thicken:**
   - Continue to cook the mixture, stirring constantly, until it thickens and becomes glossy. This should take about 5-7 minutes. Add salt to taste and adjust the consistency with a little more water if needed.
6. **Cool and Set:**
   - Once thickened, pour the sesame mixture into small individual serving dishes or a shallow container. Let it cool to room temperature, then refrigerate to set for at least 1 hour or until firm.
7. **Serve Gomadofu:**
   - To serve, carefully unmold the chilled Gomadofu onto individual plates.
   - Serve with soy sauce and a small amount of wasabi on the side for dipping.
   - Garnish with thinly sliced green onions if desired.

Notes:

- **Texture and Consistency:** Gomadofu should have a smooth and slightly firm texture, similar to tofu but with a distinct sesame flavor.

- **Variations:** Some recipes may include a touch of mirin (sweet rice wine) or sugar for added sweetness.
- **Traditional Tools:** While a food processor can be used for grinding sesame seeds, using a suribachi (Japanese mortar and pestle) traditionally helps achieve a smoother texture and enhances the dish's authenticity.

Enjoy this Gomadofu as part of a Shojin Ryori meal, along with other dishes such as vegetable tempura, pickles (tsukemono), and miso soup. It's a wonderful example of the mindfulness and simplicity that defines Buddhist vegetarian cuisine, honoring both tradition and healthful eating.

Dashi (Japanese Soup Stock)

Ingredients:

- 4 cups water
- 1 piece kombu (dried kelp), about 4 inches square

Instructions:

1. **Prepare the Kombu:**
   - Gently wipe the kombu with a damp cloth to clean it, but do not scrub off the white powder (umami-rich compounds).
2. **Soak the Kombu:**
   - Place the kombu in a pot with 4 cups of water and let it soak for at least 30 minutes. This allows the umami flavors to infuse into the water.
3. **Heat the Kombu:**
   - Place the pot over medium heat. Just before the water comes to a boil, remove the kombu from the pot. Do not let it boil, as boiling can release bitter flavors.
4. **Use the Kombu Dashi:**
   - Kombu dashi is now ready to use as a base for vegetarian soups and sauces. It has a subtle, slightly sweet flavor with a pronounced umami taste.

2. Katsuobushi Dashi (Bonito Flakes Stock)

Ingredients:

- 4 cups water
- 1 piece kombu (about 4 inches square)
- 1 cup katsuobushi (bonito flakes)

Instructions:

1. **Prepare the Kombu:**
   - Clean the kombu as mentioned above.
2. **Make Kombu Dashi:**
   - Follow steps 1 and 2 of the Kombu Dashi recipe.
3. **Add Bonito Flakes:**
   - Just as the water with kombu starts to boil, remove the pot from heat and add the bonito flakes.
4. **Steep the Bonito Flakes:**
   - Let the bonito flakes steep in the hot water for about 5 minutes. They will sink to the bottom of the pot.
5. **Strain the Dashi:**
   - After steeping, strain the dashi through a fine mesh sieve lined with cheesecloth or a paper towel. This will remove the bonito flakes and any solids.

6. **Use the Katsuobushi Dashi:**
   - Katsuobushi dashi is now ready to use. It has a deeper umami flavor compared to kombu dashi and is commonly used in traditional Japanese dishes like miso soup and noodle broths.

Tips:

- **Storage:** Dashi can be stored in the refrigerator for up to 3 days. It can also be frozen in ice cube trays and stored for longer periods, ready to be used as needed.
- **Enhancements:** Some variations of dashi include adding dried shiitake mushrooms for a vegetarian dashi or combining both kombu and katsuobushi for a richer flavor profile.

By mastering the art of making dashi, you can elevate your Japanese cooking and enjoy the authentic flavors of traditional dishes at home. Dashi forms the foundation of umami in Japanese cuisine, enhancing the overall taste and depth of various dishes.

Mitarashi Dango (Sweet Rice Dumplings)

Ingredients:

- 1 cup shiratamako (sweet rice flour) or mochiko (glutinous rice flour)
- 1/2 cup water (adjust as needed)
- Bamboo skewers

For the Mitarashi Sauce:

- 1/4 cup soy sauce
- 1/4 cup mirin (sweet rice wine)
- 2 tablespoons sugar
- 1/2 cup water
- 1 tablespoon katakuriko (potato starch) or cornstarch mixed with 1 tablespoon water (optional, for thickening)

Instructions:

1. **Prepare the Dango Dough:**
    - In a mixing bowl, combine the shiratamako or mochiko flour with water. Mix well using a spoon or your hands until a smooth dough forms. Adjust the amount of water if needed to achieve a smooth, slightly sticky consistency.
2. **Form the Dango Balls:**
    - Divide the dough into small pieces and roll each piece into balls about 1 inch in diameter. You should get around 12-15 dango balls depending on the size.
3. **Boil the Dango:**
    - Bring a large pot of water to a boil. Gently drop the dango balls into the boiling water.
    - Cook the dango balls for about 2-3 minutes, or until they float to the surface and are cooked through. Use a slotted spoon to transfer them to a bowl of cold water to stop the cooking process.
4. **Skewer the Dango:**
    - Thread 3-4 dango balls onto each bamboo skewer, leaving a little space between each ball.
5. **Make the Mitarashi Sauce:**
    - In a saucepan, combine soy sauce, mirin, sugar, and water. Bring the mixture to a boil over medium heat, stirring constantly to dissolve the sugar.
    - Optional: If you prefer a thicker sauce, mix katakuriko or cornstarch with water in a small bowl until smooth. Stir the starch mixture into the saucepan and cook until the sauce thickens slightly.
6. **Coat the Dango:**
    - Brush or drizzle the mitarashi sauce generously over the skewered dango balls, coating them evenly.
7. **Grill or Broil (Optional):**

- To enhance the flavor, you can grill the coated dango skewers over medium heat on a grill pan or broil them in the oven for a few minutes until the sauce caramelizes slightly. Watch closely to prevent burning.

8. **Serve:**
   - Arrange the mitarashi dango skewers on a plate and drizzle any remaining sauce over them.
   - Enjoy mitarashi dango warm or at room temperature. They can be served as a dessert or snack.

Tips:

- **Texture:** Adjust the water amount when making the dough to achieve the right consistency. The dough should be smooth and slightly sticky.
- **Sauce Variations:** Some recipes use different ratios of soy sauce, mirin, and sugar for the mitarashi sauce. Adjust according to your taste preferences.
- **Storage:** Leftover mitarashi dango can be stored in an airtight container in the refrigerator. Reheat gently in the microwave or enjoy cold.

Mitarashi dango is a delightful treat that combines the chewiness of rice dumplings with the sweet and savory flavors of the soy-based glaze. It's a wonderful introduction to traditional Japanese sweets and perfect for sharing with friends and family.

Hambagu (Japanese Hamburger Steak)

Ingredients:

- 1 cup shiratamako (sweet rice flour) or mochiko (glutinous rice flour)
- 1/2 cup water (adjust as needed)
- Bamboo skewers

For the Mitarashi Sauce:

- 1/4 cup soy sauce
- 1/4 cup mirin (sweet rice wine)
- 2 tablespoons sugar
- 1/2 cup water
- 1 tablespoon katakuriko (potato starch) or cornstarch mixed with 1 tablespoon water (optional, for thickening)

Instructions:

1. **Prepare the Dango Dough:**
   - In a mixing bowl, combine the shiratamako or mochiko flour with water. Mix well using a spoon or your hands until a smooth dough forms. Adjust the amount of water if needed to achieve a smooth, slightly sticky consistency.
2. **Form the Dango Balls:**
   - Divide the dough into small pieces and roll each piece into balls about 1 inch in diameter. You should get around 12-15 dango balls depending on the size.
3. **Boil the Dango:**
   - Bring a large pot of water to a boil. Gently drop the dango balls into the boiling water.
   - Cook the dango balls for about 2-3 minutes, or until they float to the surface and are cooked through. Use a slotted spoon to transfer them to a bowl of cold water to stop the cooking process.
4. **Skewer the Dango:**
   - Thread 3-4 dango balls onto each bamboo skewer, leaving a little space between each ball.
5. **Make the Mitarashi Sauce:**
   - In a saucepan, combine soy sauce, mirin, sugar, and water. Bring the mixture to a boil over medium heat, stirring constantly to dissolve the sugar.
   - Optional: If you prefer a thicker sauce, mix katakuriko or cornstarch with water in a small bowl until smooth. Stir the starch mixture into the saucepan and cook until the sauce thickens slightly.
6. **Coat the Dango:**
   - Brush or drizzle the mitarashi sauce generously over the skewered dango balls, coating them evenly.
7. **Grill or Broil (Optional):**

- To enhance the flavor, you can grill the coated dango skewers over medium heat on a grill pan or broil them in the oven for a few minutes until the sauce caramelizes slightly. Watch closely to prevent burning.

8. **Serve:**
     - Arrange the mitarashi dango skewers on a plate and drizzle any remaining sauce over them.
     - Enjoy mitarashi dango warm or at room temperature. They can be served as a dessert or snack.

Tips:

- **Texture:** Adjust the water amount when making the dough to achieve the right consistency. The dough should be smooth and slightly sticky.
- **Sauce Variations:** Some recipes use different ratios of soy sauce, mirin, and sugar for the mitarashi sauce. Adjust according to your taste preferences.
- **Storage:** Leftover mitarashi dango can be stored in an airtight container in the refrigerator. Reheat gently in the microwave or enjoy cold.

Mitarashi dango is a delightful treat that combines the chewiness of rice dumplings with the sweet and savory flavors of the soy-based glaze. It's a wonderful introduction to traditional Japanese sweets and perfect for sharing with friends and family.

Kaiseki Ryori (Traditional Multi-course Meal)

Menu Overview:

1. **Sakizuke (Appetizer):**
   - Assorted small appetizers to stimulate the appetite.
2. **Hassun (Seasonal Delicacies):**
   - Seasonal ingredients and delicacies presented on a single plate.
3. **Suimono (Clear Soup):**
   - Light and clear broth with subtle flavors.
4. **Tsukuri (Sashimi):**
   - Fresh slices of raw fish or seafood.
5. **Yakimono (Grilled Dish):**
   - Grilled fish or meat seasoned simply.
6. **Mushimono (Steamed Dish):**
   - Steamed dish often featuring seafood or vegetables.
7. **Agemono (Deep-fried Dish):**
   - Lightly battered and deep-fried dish, usually seafood or vegetables.
8. **Sunomono (Vinegared Dish):**
   - Refreshing vinegared dish, typically featuring vegetables or seafood.
9. **Gohan (Rice Dish):**
   - Steamed rice, often served towards the end of the meal.
10. **Dessert:**
    - Seasonal fruits or traditional Japanese sweets (wagashi).

Recipe:

1. Sakizuke (Assorted Appetizers):

- **Ingredients:**
  - Edamame (steamed young soybeans)
  - Agedashi tofu (deep-fried tofu in dashi broth)
  - Goma-ae (blanched vegetables dressed in sesame sauce)
  - Tsukemono (Japanese pickles)

2. Hassun (Seasonal Delicacies):

- **Ingredients:**
  - Slices of seasonal sashimi (such as tuna, salmon, or sea bream)
  - Grilled or steamed seasonal vegetables (e.g., bamboo shoots, mushrooms)
  - Tamagoyaki (Japanese rolled omelette)
  - Simmered dish (e.g., braised fish or vegetables)

3. Suimono (Clear Soup):

- **Ingredients:**
  - Dashi stock (made from kombu and bonito flakes)
  - Seasonal ingredients like tofu, mushrooms, or mitsuba (Japanese wild parsley)
- **Instructions:**
  - Heat the dashi stock and add the seasonal ingredients. Simmer gently until the flavors meld. Season lightly with soy sauce and mirin if needed.

4. Tsukuri (Sashimi):

- **Ingredients:**
  - Fresh sashimi-grade fish (tuna, salmon, yellowtail), thinly sliced
  - Wasabi (Japanese horseradish)
  - Soy sauce
- **Instructions:**
  - Arrange the slices of sashimi on a serving plate. Serve with small dishes of soy sauce and freshly grated wasabi.

5. Yakimono (Grilled Dish):

- **Ingredients:**
  - Grilled fish (such as mackerel or sea bass) or yakitori (grilled chicken skewers)
  - Light seasoning with salt or a touch of soy sauce and mirin
- **Instructions:**
  - Grill the fish or meat until cooked through, with a lightly charred exterior. Serve hot.

6. Mushimono (Steamed Dish):

- **Ingredients:**
  - Chawanmushi (savory egg custard) with seasonal ingredients like shrimp, mushrooms, and ginkgo nuts
- **Instructions:**
  - Steam the chawanmushi until set. Serve warm in individual cups or bowls.

7. Agemono (Deep-fried Dish):

- **Ingredients:**
  - Tempura (assorted vegetables and seafood lightly battered and deep-fried)
  - Tentsuyu (tempura dipping sauce)
- **Instructions:**
  - Prepare the tempura by lightly battering and frying seasonal vegetables and seafood. Serve hot with tentsuyu dipping sauce.

8. Sunomono (Vinegared Dish):

- **Ingredients:**

- - Sunomono salad with thinly sliced cucumber, wakame seaweed, and shrimp or crab
    - Sweet vinegar dressing
  - **Instructions:**
    - Mix the ingredients for the sunomono salad and toss with the sweet vinegar dressing. Serve chilled.

9. Gohan (Rice Dish):

- **Ingredients:**
  - Steamed Japanese rice (uruchimai)
- **Instructions:**
  - Serve steamed rice in individual bowls.

10. Dessert:

- **Ingredients:**
  - Seasonal fruits (such as persimmons, strawberries, or melon)
  - Traditional Japanese sweets (wagashi) like mochi or dorayaki (red bean pancake)
- **Instructions:**
  - Serve seasonal fruits or traditional sweets as a light and refreshing end to the meal.

Tips:

- **Presentation:** Arrange each dish with attention to detail and aesthetics, as presentation is crucial in Kaiseki Ryori.
- **Seasonality:** Use fresh, seasonal ingredients to highlight the flavors and textures of each course.
- **Balance:** Aim for a balanced meal with a variety of flavors and cooking techniques represented.
- **Enjoyment:** Kaiseki Ryori is not just about eating but also about appreciating the craftsmanship and cultural significance behind each dish.

Preparing a Kaiseki Ryori meal at home allows you to experience the essence of Japanese culinary artistry and hospitality. Adjust the recipes and courses based on seasonal availability and personal preferences to create your own memorable Kaiseki-style dining experience.

Hamachi Kama (Yellowtail Collar)

Ingredients:

- 1 or 2 Hamachi Kama (yellowtail collars), depending on the size and number of servings
- Salt, to taste
- Lemon wedges, for serving
- Optional: soy sauce, ponzu sauce, or grated daikon radish for serving

Instructions:

1. **Preparation:**
   - Thaw the Hamachi Kama if frozen, and pat dry with paper towels. This helps to ensure crispy skin when cooking.
2. **Seasoning:**
   - Sprinkle both sides of the Hamachi Kama generously with salt. Allow it to sit for about 10-15 minutes to enhance the flavor.
3. **Grilling:**
   - Preheat your grill to medium-high heat. If using a charcoal grill, arrange the coals for direct heat grilling.
4. **Grill the Hamachi Kama:**
   - Place the Hamachi Kama on the grill, skin-side down first. Grill for about 5-7 minutes on each side, or until the skin is crispy and golden brown. Use tongs to carefully flip the collar to grill the other side.
5. **Check Doneness:**
   - The fish should be opaque and flake easily with a fork when done. Be careful not to overcook, as yellowtail can dry out quickly.
6. **Serve:**
   - Transfer the grilled Hamachi Kama to a serving plate. Serve hot with lemon wedges on the side for squeezing over the fish.
7. **Optional Serving Suggestions:**
   - Serve with soy sauce, ponzu sauce, or grated daikon radish to complement the flavors of the Hamachi Kama.

Tips:

- **Grilling Variations:** If you don't have a grill, you can also broil the Hamachi Kama in the oven. Preheat the broiler, place the fish on a broiler pan, and broil for about 5-7 minutes on each side until cooked through.
- **Flavor Enhancements:** Feel free to experiment with additional seasonings such as black pepper, garlic powder, or a sprinkle of citrus zest before grilling.
- **Serving Size:** One Hamachi Kama can typically serve 1-2 people, depending on the size and appetite.

Hamachi Kama is prized for its tender, juicy meat and crispy skin, making it a delightful dish enjoyed in both casual and upscale settings. It's perfect for seafood lovers looking to explore authentic Japanese flavors at home.

Chirashizushi (Scattered Sushi)

Ingredients:

- 2 cups sushi rice
- 2 1/2 cups water
- 5 tablespoons rice vinegar
- 2 tablespoons sugar
- 1 teaspoon salt
- Assorted toppings such as:
    - Sashimi (e.g., tuna, salmon, yellowtail)
    - Cooked shrimp
    - Cucumber, thinly sliced
    - Avocado, sliced
    - Tamagoyaki (Japanese rolled omelette), thinly sliced
    - Shredded nori (seaweed)
    - Pickled ginger (gari)
    - Wasabi
    - Sesame seeds (black or white)
    - Edamame beans
    - Radish sprouts (kaiware)
    - Thinly sliced lemon or lime

Instructions:

1. **Prepare the Sushi Rice:**
    - Rinse the sushi rice under cold water until the water runs clear. This removes excess starch.
    - In a rice cooker or pot, combine the rinsed rice with 2 1/2 cups of water. Cook the rice according to your rice cooker instructions or bring to a boil, then reduce heat to low and simmer, covered, for about 15-20 minutes until the rice is cooked and tender.
2. **Season the Rice:**
    - In a small bowl, mix the rice vinegar, sugar, and salt until dissolved.
    - Transfer the cooked rice to a large wooden or glass bowl (traditionally used to prevent the rice from absorbing unwanted flavors). Gradually add the vinegar mixture to the rice while gently folding it in with a rice paddle or spatula. Continue folding and fanning the rice to cool it down to room temperature.
3. **Prepare the Toppings:**
    - Prepare your choice of toppings. Slice the sashimi into thin strips or bite-sized pieces. Cook and slice the shrimp. Cut the cucumber, avocado, and tamagoyaki into thin slices.
4. **Assemble the Chirashizushi:**

- Transfer the seasoned sushi rice to a large serving bowl or platter, spreading it out evenly.
- Arrange the toppings decoratively over the rice. Start with larger items like sashimi and shrimp, and then fill in with smaller items like cucumber, avocado, and tamagoyaki.
- Scatter nori shreds, pickled ginger, wasabi, sesame seeds, edamame beans, and radish sprouts over the top for added flavor and texture.

5. **Serve:**
   - Serve Chirashizushi at room temperature. It can be enjoyed as-is or with soy sauce and additional wasabi on the side.
   - Garnish with thinly sliced lemon or lime for extra freshness.

Tips:

- **Variety:** Feel free to customize your Chirashizushi with your favorite seafood and vegetables. It's a versatile dish that can accommodate seasonal ingredients and personal preferences.
- **Preparation:** Prepare the sushi rice and toppings ahead of time for easier assembly just before serving.
- **Presentation:** Chirashizushi is meant to be visually appealing, so take care with arranging the toppings in an attractive and colorful manner.

Chirashizushi is a delightful way to enjoy sushi flavors without the need for rolling or shaping individual pieces, making it accessible for home cooks and perfect for sharing with family and friends.

Yakisoba (Stir-Fried Noodles)

Ingredients:

- 200g yakisoba noodles (or substitute with ramen noodles or even spaghetti)
- 1 small onion, thinly sliced
- 1 carrot, julienned or thinly sliced
- 1 small bell pepper (any color), thinly sliced
- 1 cup cabbage, thinly shredded
- 1/2 cup bean sprouts (optional)
- 2-3 green onions, chopped
- 1/2 cup thinly sliced pork belly or chicken breast (optional)
- Vegetable oil, for cooking

For the Yakisoba Sauce:

- 3 tablespoons Worcestershire sauce
- 2 tablespoons oyster sauce
- 2 tablespoons soy sauce
- 1 tablespoon ketchup
- 1 tablespoon sugar
- 1/4 cup water

Optional Toppings:

- Aonori (dried seaweed flakes)
- Beni shoga (pickled ginger)
- Katsuobushi (bonito flakes)

Instructions:

1. **Prepare the Yakisoba Noodles:**
    - If using packaged yakisoba noodles, follow the package instructions to cook them. Usually, this involves briefly boiling the noodles, then draining and rinsing them under cold water to remove excess starch. If using other noodles like ramen or spaghetti, cook according to package instructions and drain well.
2. **Make the Yakisoba Sauce:**
    - In a small bowl, mix together Worcestershire sauce, oyster sauce, soy sauce, ketchup, sugar, and water. Stir until well combined. Adjust sweetness or saltiness to your preference by adding more sugar or soy sauce.
3. **Stir-Fry the Ingredients:**
    - Heat 1-2 tablespoons of vegetable oil in a large pan or wok over medium-high heat.
    - Add the sliced onion and stir-fry for 1-2 minutes until translucent.

- Add the sliced pork or chicken (if using) and cook until browned and cooked through.
- Add the carrot, bell pepper, cabbage, and bean sprouts (if using). Stir-fry for another 2-3 minutes until the vegetables are slightly tender but still crisp.

4. **Add the Noodles and Sauce:**
   - Add the cooked noodles to the pan or wok. Toss everything together using tongs or chopsticks to combine well.
5. **Add the Yakisoba Sauce:**
   - Pour the prepared yakisoba sauce over the noodles and vegetables. Continue to stir-fry for another 2-3 minutes, ensuring that the noodles are evenly coated with the sauce and heated through.
6. **Finish and Serve:**
   - Taste and adjust seasoning if needed (you can add more soy sauce or a pinch of salt if desired).
   - Stir in chopped green onions and cook for another minute.
   - Serve the yakisoba hot, garnished with optional toppings like aonori, beni shoga, and katsuobushi.

Tips:

- **Noodle Substitutions:** If you can't find yakisoba noodles, you can use ramen noodles or even spaghetti as a substitute.
- **Vegetable Variations:** Feel free to add or substitute vegetables based on what you have or prefer. Mushrooms, snow peas, and bamboo shoots are also common additions.
- **Protein Options:** Aside from pork or chicken, you can also use shrimp, tofu, or omit the meat altogether for a vegetarian version.

Yakisoba is a versatile and comforting dish that's perfect for a quick weeknight meal or a casual gathering with friends. It's easy to customize to suit your tastes and a great way to introduce Japanese flavors into your cooking repertoire.

Matcha (Green Tea) Desserts

Matcha Cheesecake Bars

Ingredients:

For the Crust:

- 1 1/2 cups graham cracker crumbs (about 10-12 graham crackers)
- 1/4 cup granulated sugar
- 1/2 cup unsalted butter, melted

For the Matcha Cheesecake Filling:

- 16 oz (450g) cream cheese, softened (2 packages)
- 1/2 cup granulated sugar
- 2 tablespoons all-purpose flour
- 2 large eggs
- 1/4 cup sour cream
- 1/4 cup heavy cream
- 2 tablespoons matcha powder
- 1 teaspoon vanilla extract

Instructions:

1. **Preheat the Oven:**
   - Preheat your oven to 325°F (160°C). Grease or line a 9x9 inch (23x23 cm) baking pan with parchment paper, leaving an overhang for easy removal.
2. **Make the Crust:**
   - In a mixing bowl, combine the graham cracker crumbs, sugar, and melted butter. Mix until the crumbs are evenly coated with butter.
   - Press the mixture firmly and evenly into the bottom of the prepared baking pan.
   - Bake the crust in the preheated oven for 10 minutes. Remove from the oven and set aside to cool slightly while preparing the filling.
3. **Make the Matcha Cheesecake Filling:**
   - In a large bowl, beat the softened cream cheese until smooth using a hand mixer or stand mixer.
   - Add the granulated sugar and flour, and beat until combined and creamy.
   - Add the eggs, one at a time, mixing well after each addition.
   - Mix in the sour cream, heavy cream, matcha powder, and vanilla extract until smooth and evenly combined. Scrape down the sides of the bowl as needed to ensure everything is incorporated.
4. **Assemble and Bake:**
   - Pour the matcha cheesecake filling over the cooled crust in the baking pan.
   - Smooth the top with a spatula to create an even layer.

5. **Bake the Cheesecake:**
   - Bake in the preheated oven for 35-40 minutes, or until the edges are set and the center is slightly jiggly.
   - Remove from the oven and let the cheesecake cool completely in the pan on a wire rack.
6. **Chill and Serve:**
   - Once cooled to room temperature, refrigerate the cheesecake bars for at least 4 hours or overnight to set completely.
   - Use the parchment paper overhang to lift the cheesecake out of the pan. Cut into bars using a sharp knife.
7. **Serve and Enjoy:**
   - Serve the matcha cheesecake bars chilled. Optionally, dust with additional matcha powder or decorate with whipped cream and fresh berries.

Notes:

- **Storage:** Store leftover matcha cheesecake bars in an airtight container in the refrigerator for up to 4-5 days.
- **Variations:** Feel free to adjust the amount of matcha powder based on your preference for a stronger or milder matcha flavor.
- **Garnish:** Enhance the presentation with a sprinkle of powdered sugar or a drizzle of chocolate sauce.

These Matcha Cheesecake Bars are creamy, luscious, and have a beautiful green tea flavor that pairs wonderfully with the richness of the cheesecake. They make a delightful dessert for any occasion, combining the elegance of matcha with the indulgence of cheesecake.

Wagashi (Traditional Japanese Sweets)

Ichigo Daifuku (Strawberry Mochi)

Ingredients:

- 6-8 fresh strawberries, washed and hulled
- 200g Shiratamako (sweet glutinous rice flour) or Mochiko (sweet rice flour)
- 40g granulated sugar
- 160ml water
- Potato starch or cornstarch, for dusting
- 200g sweet red bean paste (anko)

Instructions:

1. **Prepare the Strawberries:**
    - Wash the strawberries and remove the stems (hulls). Pat them dry with paper towels and set aside.
2. **Make the Sweet Red Bean Paste (Anko):**
    - If you prefer homemade anko, cook 200g of adzuki beans with water until soft, drain, and mash. Add 100g of sugar and cook on low heat until thickened. Let it cool completely.
3. **Prepare the Mochi Dough:**
    - In a microwave-safe bowl, mix Shiratamako (or Mochiko) and granulated sugar.
    - Gradually add water, stirring until smooth and there are no lumps.
4. **Microwave the Mochi Dough:**
    - Cover the bowl loosely with plastic wrap or a microwave-safe lid.
    - Microwave on high for 1 minute. Remove from the microwave and stir well with a wet spatula or spoon.
    - Microwave for another 1 minute. The dough should be translucent and sticky.
5. **Forming the Daifuku:**
    - Dust a clean surface with potato starch or cornstarch.
    - Transfer the mochi dough onto the dusted surface. Be careful as it will be hot.
    - Divide the dough into 6-8 equal portions, depending on the number of strawberries.
    - Flatten each portion into a round disc about 3 inches (7-8 cm) in diameter.
6. **Assemble the Ichigo Daifuku:**
    - Place a small amount (about 1 tablespoon) of sweet red bean paste (anko) in the center of each mochi disc.
    - Press a strawberry (hulled side down) onto the anko filling.
    - Gather the edges of the mochi disc around the strawberry and pinch to seal. Twist and pinch the excess dough at the top to close.
7. **Serve and Enjoy:**
    - Serve the Ichigo Daifuku immediately or store in an airtight container in the refrigerator. Enjoy these delightful Wagashi treats with tea!

Notes:

- **Storage:** Ichigo Daifuku are best enjoyed fresh but can be stored in the refrigerator for up to 1-2 days. The mochi texture will become firmer over time.
- **Variations:** You can experiment with different fillings such as other fruits, flavored anko (like matcha or chestnut), or even custard.

Making Wagashi at home allows you to appreciate the delicate flavors and textures of these traditional Japanese sweets. Enjoy the process of creating these Ichigo Daifuku and savor the unique combination of mochi, anko, and fresh strawberry!

Sunomono (Cucumber Salad)

Ingredients:

- 1 large cucumber (Japanese or English cucumber works well)
- 1/2 teaspoon salt
- 2 tablespoons rice vinegar
- 1 tablespoon sugar
- 1/4 teaspoon soy sauce (optional)
- 1/2 teaspoon sesame seeds, toasted (optional)
- Thinly sliced nori (seaweed) for garnish (optional)

Instructions:

1. **Prepare the Cucumber:**
   - Wash the cucumber thoroughly. If using a regular cucumber with a thicker skin, you can peel alternating strips for a decorative effect. Slice the cucumber thinly into rounds using a sharp knife or a mandoline slicer.
2. **Salt the Cucumber:**
   - Place the sliced cucumbers in a bowl and sprinkle with 1/2 teaspoon of salt. Toss gently to coat the cucumbers evenly. Let them sit for about 10-15 minutes. This helps to draw out excess water from the cucumbers.
3. **Make the Dressing:**
   - In a separate small bowl, combine rice vinegar and sugar. Stir until the sugar is completely dissolved. You can adjust the sweetness by adding more or less sugar according to your preference.
   - If desired, add a splash of soy sauce for added depth of flavor.
4. **Assemble the Sunomono:**
   - After 10-15 minutes, squeeze the cucumber slices gently to remove excess water. Transfer the cucumbers to a clean bowl.
   - Pour the dressing over the cucumbers and toss gently to coat evenly.
5. **Chill and Serve:**
   - Cover the bowl with plastic wrap and refrigerate for at least 30 minutes to allow the flavors to meld together and the cucumbers to marinate.
6. **Garnish and Serve:**
   - Before serving, sprinkle toasted sesame seeds over the cucumber salad for added crunch and nutty flavor.
   - Optionally, garnish with thinly sliced nori (seaweed) for a traditional touch and extra umami.
7. **Enjoy:**
   - Serve Sunomono chilled as a refreshing side dish or appetizer alongside your favorite Japanese dishes. It pairs particularly well with sushi, sashimi, or grilled meats.

Notes:

- **Variations:** Sunomono can be customized by adding other ingredients such as thinly sliced carrots, radishes, or seafood like shrimp or crab sticks.
- **Make Ahead:** You can prepare Sunomono ahead of time and store it in the refrigerator for up to a day. The flavors will continue to develop, making it even more delicious.

Sunomono is a simple yet elegant dish that showcases the freshness of cucumbers and the delicate balance of sweet and tangy flavors. It's a perfect addition to your Japanese meal or as a light and healthy snack.

Dorayaki (Red Bean Pancakes)

Ingredients:

For the Pancakes:

- 2 large eggs
- 1/2 cup (100g) granulated sugar
- 1 tablespoon honey or maple syrup
- 1 teaspoon vanilla extract
- 1/2 cup (120ml) milk
- 1 cup (120g) all-purpose flour
- 1 teaspoon baking powder
- Oil or butter for cooking

For the Filling:

- 1 cup sweet red bean paste (anko)

Instructions:

1. **Prepare the Pancake Batter:**
   - In a mixing bowl, whisk together eggs, sugar, honey (or maple syrup), and vanilla extract until smooth and creamy.
   - Add milk and mix until well combined.
   - Sift in the flour and baking powder. Gently fold the dry ingredients into the wet ingredients until just combined. Do not overmix; a few lumps are okay.
   - Let the batter rest for about 10-15 minutes.
2. **Cook the Pancakes:**
   - Heat a non-stick skillet or griddle over medium heat. Lightly grease the surface with oil or butter.
   - Pour about 1/4 cup of batter onto the skillet for each pancake, spreading it slightly into a round shape (about 4 inches/10 cm in diameter).
   - Cook until bubbles start to form on the surface of the pancake and the edges begin to set, about 2-3 minutes.
   - Flip the pancakes carefully with a spatula and cook for another 1-2 minutes until golden brown and cooked through.
   - Transfer the cooked pancakes to a plate and cover with a clean kitchen towel to keep them warm and moist. Repeat with the remaining batter.
3. **Assemble the Dorayaki:**
   - Once the pancakes are cool enough to handle but still warm, spread a generous amount of sweet red bean paste (anko) onto the center of one pancake.
   - Place another pancake on top, pressing gently to sandwich the filling between the two pancakes.
4. **Serve and Enjoy:**

- Serve Dorayaki warm or at room temperature. They are best enjoyed fresh, but leftovers can be stored in an airtight container in the refrigerator for a day or two.

Notes:

- **Red Bean Paste (Anko):** You can use store-bought sweet red bean paste (anko) or make your own. To make homemade anko, cook adzuki beans with sugar until soft and mash them into a smooth paste.
- **Variations:** Dorayaki can be filled with other fillings such as custard, whipped cream with fruits, or even Nutella for a modern twist.
- **Authenticity:** Traditional Dorayaki has a slight chewiness to the pancakes. If you prefer a softer texture, you can add a little more milk to the batter.

Dorayaki is a delightful treat that combines the fluffy texture of pancakes with the sweet richness of red bean paste. It's perfect for breakfast, dessert, or as a snack with tea or coffee. Enjoy making and savoring these homemade Dorayaki with your loved ones!

www.ingramcontent.com/pod-product-compliance
Lightning Source LLC
LaVergne TN
LVHW081557060526
838201LV00054B/1930